SUNDAY
in the
PARK
with
GEORGE

Music and Lyrics by
STEPHEN SONDHEIM

Book by
JAMES LAPINE

Introduction by André Bishop

APPLAUSE
THEATRE BOOK PUBLISHERS

Sunday in the Park with George

Copyright © 1991, by Applause Theatre Book Publishers. Book Copyright © 1984 by James Lapine.

Music and Lyrics Copyright © 1984 by Stephen Sondheim, Revelation Music Publishing Corp. and Rilting Music, Inc. All rights reserved.

Grateful acknowledgement is made to the following for permission to include their photographs and scene and costume designs: Martha Swope Associates, Zoë Dominic Photography, Tony Straiges, Patricia Zipprodt and Ann Hould-Ward.

Drawings by Hirschfeld Copyright © 1984 by Al Hirschfeld and reproduced by special arrangement with Hirschfeld's exclusive representative, the Margo Feiden Galleries Ltd., New York.

Design by Gary Denys.

Library of Congress Cataloging-in-Publication Data
Sondheim, Stephen.
      [Sunday in the park with George. Libretto]
      Sunday in the park with George/ music and lyrics by Stephen Sondheim; book by James Lapine; introduction by Andre Bishop.
      p. cm. -- (The Applause musical library)
      Libretto.
      Discography: p.
      ISBN 1-55783-067-3 : $19.95. - ISBN 1-55783-068-1 (pbk.) : $9.95
      1. Musicals–Librettos. 2. Seurat, Georges. 1859-1891—Drama. I. Lapine, James. II. Title.
ML50.S705S8   1990   <Case>   90-981
782.1'40268–dc20   CIP
                                                                                        MN

No part of this book may be reproduced in any form without permission in writing from the publisher.

Manufactured in the United States of America

Applause Theatre & Cinema Books   Sales & Distribution:
19 West 21st Street, Suite 201   Hal Leonard Corp.
New York, NY 10010   7777 West Bluemound Road
Phone: (212) 575-9265   P.O. Box 13819
Fax: (212) 575-9270   Milwaukee, WI 53213
Email: info@applausepub.com   Phone: (414) 774-3630
Internet: www.applausepub.com   Fax: (414) 774-3259
                                                               Email: halinfo@halleonard.com
                                                               Internet: www.halleonard.com

Applause books are available through your local bookstore, or you may order at www.applausepub.com or call Music Dispatch at 800-637-2852.

First Applause Printing, 1991

"Sunday in the Park with George"
was originally produced on Broadway by
The Shubert Organization and Emmanuel Azenberg
By arrangement with
Playwrights Horizons

Playwrights Horizons, Inc., New York City,
Produced the original production of
"Sunday in the Park with George"
in 1983

CONTENTS

Introduction by André Bishop   1

Sunday in the Park with George   9

Additional Lyrics   187

Major Productions   201

Selected Discography   213

Illustrations:

     Drawings by Hirschfeld   6-8

     Production photographs   91-120

     Set and costume designs by Tony Straiges,

         Patricia Zipprodt and Ann-Hould Ward   175-186

INTRODUCTION

I did a great deal of reading about *Sunday in the Park with George* before I sat down to write this introduction. I discovered that masses of articles, interviews, and essays had been written about this landmark musical since its opening on Broadway in April of 1984. I realized that I had nothing especially new to say about the show—Sondheim's use of "chord clusters," Lapine's avoidance of Latin root words and contractions in an effort to simulate 19th Century French speech patterns, the trials and tribulations of getting the second act into shape and so on—all of these have been well documented.

I then did something you are about to do: I read the text. I was deeply moved. I found the sheer audacity of the *idea* of the show amazing. Imagine a musical in which the first act breathes dramatic life into one of the great works of late 19th Century painting. Then try to top Act One with a second act that takes place a hundred years later and deals satirically with the contemporary art world and then goes on to chronicle the sadness of a young artist who has lost his way in it.

Sunday in the Park with George is a very personal show and so it seems appropriate that this introduction be personal too. The show meant a great deal to its creators, indeed to all who worked on it. My presence in these pages can be explained because it was my theater, Playwrights Horizons, that commissioned the piece initially from James Lapine and then gave it its first home and its first production prior to the run on Broadway. My recollections of a hectic, exhilarating time are happy ones, although Playwrights Horizons had never produced a musical on such a large scale before. Enormous amounts of time and energy went into organizing ourselves to go into rehearsal for a piece that we knew very little about—there was a first act with a number of songs and a sketch of a second act. That was it.

People would say to me, "Why are you putting on such an elaborate production of something that is only half-written?" Indeed, though we called the event a "workshop" and believe me it was a *workshop*, we had to raise a great deal of money to do it and a lot of that money went into costumes and sets. It seems to me, as I look back, that we were always having benefits and that I was always lugging around color reproductions of *La Grande Jatte* to show to prospective donors! In any event, I believed that if you were doing a show about vision and creation and if the *event* was the recreation of a painting of people in a French park in 1884, you couldn't effectively "workshop" the visuals with women in rehearsal skirts, men in leotards, and a black velour surround. You had to do it full out or not at all.

One of the highlights of our production and of the show turned out to be the end of Act One when Seurat artfully arranges the various groups of squabbling Parisians into a perfect and harmonious picture. There was something about the scale of the final image that related beautifully to the dimensions of our small theater space. When everyone on stage sang the final three "Sundays," and the horn played, and the picture was complete and frozen, and the blank canvas that we used as a show curtain came in—well, it was a perfect blend for the ear and the eye. And most nights the audience (even some of the ancient ones who occasionally nodded off) would cheer and stomp and scream their approval. Though the show was infinitely better and more complete on Broadway, I always felt that the Act One finale worked best at Playwrights Horizons. It was literally and beautifully overpowering.

2

When we began performances in July of 1983, we had most of a first act ("Everybody Loves Louis," "Beautiful," and "Finishing the Hat" were added during our run) and hardly any Act Two. So we decided to only perform the first act—it was, after all, a fairly complete unit—and to add Act Two when the authors were ready. We hoped our loyal subscription audience would accept this in the spirit of a "work-in-progress," and they did. Part of the reason they did had to do with the speeches I felt I should give before each performance, explaining what we were up to in as inspiring a fashion as possible and then casually mentioning that Act Two wasn't quite ready and that we were sparing them great torment by not performing it that night. Actually, we only performed it three times!

People who know me know that I'll do anything to avoid having to speak in public, but such was my fate those muggy summer nights in 1983. When I look back on it, though, I wonder if I was able to get the audience on our side for no other reason than they felt sorry for me because I appeared to be so nervous. Ira Weitzman, our Musical Theater Program Director, was much more at ease when he had to "make the speech," and by the end of the run would stroll up to the apron of the stage, wearing shorts and a T-shirt, and sort of say, "Hi, folks, guess what? No Act Two tonight, but you're gonna *love* Act One!"

The best speech night and one of the great nights of my theater life was the night "Finishing the Hat" went into the show. Mandy Patinkin had learned the music but wanted to hold onto the printed lyrics. I explained in the speech that this night was something special because a new song was being added and that Seurat would, at one point, be holding some sheets of music. An audience loves being in on something for the first time. When Mandy picked up the music and sang the song—so carefully and lovingly—and the song turned out to be deeply personal, layered with

3

meaning and metaphor, and beautifully spun out, we all felt that we had entered musical theater heaven. And we had. Even today I run into people who claim they saw the show the night "Finishing the Hat" went in and that it was a rare and special occasion.

Playwrights Horizons believes that opportunities create and sustain artists, and we felt that the best thing we could do for Sondheim and Lapine was to step back and give them a chance to discover their show. I wanted them to be free to do what they wanted without any kind of management pressure, without any kind of publicity or review, and most of all, without any kind of fear. I felt that they were onto something important, and I knew that the collaboration between the two men was new and at an early and delicate stage. Stephen Sondheim was working with a different partner for the first time in years, and he had never really worked in a non-profit situation in New York. Everyone at Playwrights Horizons wanted him to find us at our best and to work happily under a different system of creating shows than the traditional Broadway one.

Because I am writing this in June of 1990 when the National Endowment for the Arts in particular and non-profit arts subsidy in general are under attack, I want to note that the creative freedom that Sondheim and Lapine were given at my theater and the good advantage they took of it is directly due to funding dollars. If subsidy is taken away from theaters, especially those that deal with new, experimental, untried work, these theaters will fade away. And if this happens, there will be no venue for new work at all and any sort of new American theater will simply disappear. Artists will no longer have artistic homes away from the marketplace. What I'm trying to say is that had it not been for subsidy there would be no Playwrights Horizons and quite possibly no *Sunday in the Park with George*.

A month or so after the show closed at Playwrights Horizons, I flew to Chicago to go to the Art Institute where

4

Seurat's *A Sunday Afternoon on the Island of La Grande Jatte* hangs. I probably should have done this at the outset instead of at the end, because as I walked up the steps and got closer and closer to the treasured painting, I finally understood what it was the two authors were doing. In front of me, and massively so, was an extraordinary composition of shapes and colors and brushstrokes that reflected the work of a man obsessed with his art. Even to a jaded, late 20th Century New Yorker, who had seen countless reproductions of *La Grande Jatte* and had just done a show about it, the painting was startling and lovely and upsetting and inspiring. I stood and stared for hours, much as I imagine the authors did, until I felt I was both outside the painting and inside, and definitely part of it. There were many areas and people on the huge canvas that were not represented in the musical, and I wondered who they had been and why they were there. It must have been at this point of heightened curiosity and emotion that Lapine and Sondheim began their own search for a new form inspired by the legacy of an extraordinary artist from another century.

I am very proud of the part Playwrights Horizons played in the development of *Sunday in the Park with George*. I think the show represents what is best about the American musical theater, and it certainly came out of what is best about the non-profit theater.

André Bishop

Playwrights Horizons
June 1990

P.S. The two best and most detailed accounts of the partnership that created *Sunday in the Park with George* are to be found in the 2nd edition of Craig Zadan's *Sondheim and Co.* (Harper and Row) and Michiko Kakutani's article for *The New York Times*, reprinted in her book *The Poet at the Piano* (New York Times Books).

Bernadette Peters

Bernadette Peters and Mandy Patinkin

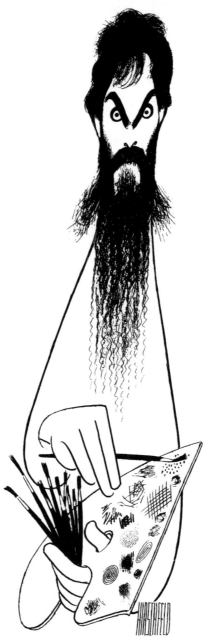

Robert Westenberg, who replaced
Mandy Patinkin in the role of George

SUNDAY
in the
PARK
with
GEORGE

For Sarah Kernochan

CAST OF CHARACTERS

ACT I

GEORGE, *an artist*
DOT, *his mistress*
OLD LADY
HER NURSE
JULES, *another artist*
YVONNE, *his wife*
LOUISE, *the daughter of Jules and Yvonne*
A BOATMAN
FRANZ, *servant to Jules and Yvonne*
FRIEDA, *cook for Jules and Yvonne, wife to Franz*
A SOLDIER
MR. *and* MRS., *an American couple*
LOUIS, *a baker*
A WOMAN *with baby carriage*
A MAN *with bicycle*
A LITTLE GIRL
CELESTE #1, *a shopgirl*
CELESTE #2, *another shopgirl*
A BOY *bathing in the river*
A YOUNG MAN *sitting on the bank*
A MAN *lying on the bank*

ACT II

GEORGE, *an artist*
MARIE, *his grandmother*
DENNIS, *a technician*
BOB GREENBERG, *the museum director*

11

NAOMI EISEN, *a composer*

HARRIET PAWLING, *a patron of the arts*

BILLY WEBSTER, *her friend*

A PHOTOGRAPHER

A MUSEUM ASSISTANT

CHARLES REDMOND, *a visiting curator*

ALEX, *an artist*

BETTY, *an artist*

LEE RANDOLPH, *the museum's publicist*

BLAIR DANIELS, *an art critic*

A WAITRESS

ELAINE, *George's former wife*

MUSICAL NUMBERS

ACT I

"Sunday in the Park with George"	DOT
"No Life"	JULES, YVONNE
"Color and Light"	DOT, GEORGE
"Gossip"	CELESTE #1, CELESTE #2, BOATMAN, NURSE, OLD LADY, JULES, YVONNE
"The Day Off"	GEORGE, NURSE, FRANZ, FRIEDA, BOATMAN, SOLDIER, CELESTE #1, CELESTE #2, YVONNE, LOUISE, JULES, LOUIS
"Everybody Loves Louis"	DOT
"Finishing the Hat"	GEORGE
"We Do Not Belong Together"	DOT, GEORGE
"Beautiful"	OLD LADY, GEORGE
"Sunday"	COMPANY

ACT II

"It's Hot Up Here"	COMPANY
Chromolume #7	GEORGE, MARIE
"Putting It Together"	GEORGE, COMPANY
"Children and Art"	MARIE
"Lesson #8"	GEORGE
"Move On"	GEORGE, DOT
"Sunday"	COMPANY

13

Act I takes place on a series of Sundays from 1884 to 1886 and alternates between a park on an island in the Seine just outside Paris and George's studio.

Act II takes place in 1984 at an American art museum and on the island.

ACT I

A white stage. White floor, slightly raked and extended in perspective. Four white portals define the space. The proscenium arch continues across the bottom as well, creating a complete frame around the stage.

GEORGE *enters downstage. He is an artist. Tall, with a dark beard, wearing a soft felt hat with a very narrow brim crushed down at the neck, and a short jacket. He looks rather intense. He sits downstage on the apron at an easel with a large drawing pad and a box of chalk. He stares momentarily at the pad before turning to the audience.*

GEORGE: White. A blank page or canvas. The challenge: bring order to the whole.
    (*Arpeggiated chord. A tree flies in stage right*)
Through design.
    (*Four arpeggiated chords. The white portals fly out and the white ground cloth comes off, revealing a grassy-green expanse and portals depicting the park scene*)
Composition.
    (*Two arpeggiated chords. A tree tracks on from stage left*)
Balance.
    (*Two arpeggiated chords. Two trees descend*)
Light.
    (*Arpeggiated chord. The lighting bumps, giving the impression of an early morning sunrise on the island of La*

17

Grande Jatte — harsh shadows and streaming golden light through the trees)
And harmony.

(The music coalesces into a theme, "Sunday," as a cut-out of a couple rises at the back of the stage. GEORGE *begins to draw, then stops suddenly and goes to the wings and brings on a young woman,* DOT. *She wears a traditional 19th-century outfit: full-length dress with bustle, etc. When he gets her downstage right, he turns her profile, then returns downstage to his easel. He begins to draw. She turns to him. Music continues under. Annoyed)*
No. Now I want you to look out at the water.

DOT: I feel foolish.

GEORGE: Why?

DOT *(Indicating bustle)*: I hate this thing.

GEORGE: Then why wear it?

DOT: Why wear it? Everyone is wearing them!

GEORGE *(Begins sketching)*: Everyone . . .

DOT: You know they are.
                    (She begins to move)

GEORGE: Stand still, please.
                    (Music stops)

DOT *(Sighs)*: I read they're even wearing them in America.

GEORGE: They are fighting Indians in America — and you cannot read.

DOT *(Defensive)*: I can read . . . a little.
                    (Pause)
Why did we have to get up so early?

GEORGE: The light.

18

DOT: Oh.
                    (GEORGE *lets out a moan*)
What's the matter?

GEORGE (*Erasing feverishly*): I hate this tree.
                    (*Arpeggio. A tree rises back into the fly space*)

DOT (*Hurt*): I thought you were drawing me.

GEORGE (*Muttering*): I am. I am. Just stand still.
    (DOT *is oblivious to the moved tree. Through the course of
    the scene the landscape can continue to change. At this
    point a sailboat begins to slide into view*)

DOT: I wish we could go sailing. I wouldn't go this early in
the day, though.

GEORGE: Could you drop your head a little, please.
                    (*She drops her head completely*)
Dot!
                    (*She looks up, giggling*)
If you wish to be a good model you must learn to concen-
trate. Hold the pose. Look out at the water.
                    (*She obliges*)
Thank you.
                    (OLD LADY *enters*)

OLD LADY: Where is that tree? (*Pause*) Nurse! NURSE!

DOT (*Startled*): My God!
                    (*Sees* OLD LADY)
She is everywhere.
        (NURSE *enters. She wears an enormous headdress*)

OLD LADY: NURSE!

NURSE: What is it, Madame?

OLD LADY: The tree. The tree. Where is our tree?

NURSE: What tree?

19

OLD LADY: The tree we always sit near. Someone has moved it.

NURSE: No one has moved it, Madame. It is right over there. Now come along —
(NURSE *attempts to help the* OLD LADY *along*)

OLD LADY: Do not push me!

NURSE: I am not pushing. I am helping.

OLD LADY: You are pushing and I do not need any help.

NURSE (*Crossing the stage*): Yes, Madame.

OLD LADY: And this is not our tree!
(*She continues her shuffle*)

NURSE: Yes, Madame.
(*She helps* OLD LADY *sit in front of tree*)

DOT: I do not envy the nurse.

GEORGE (*Under his breath*): She can read . . .

DOT (*Retaliating*): They were talking about you at La Coupole.

GEORGE: Oh.

DOT: Saying strange things . . .

GEORGE: They have so little to speak of, they must speak of me?

DOT: Were you at the zoo, George?
(*No response*)
Drawing the monkey cage?

GEORGE: Not the monkey cage.

DOT: They said they saw you.

GEORGE: The monkeys, Dot. Not the cage.

DOT (*Giggling*): It is true? Why draw monkeys?

OLD LADY: Nurse, what is that?

NURSE: What, Madame?

OLD LADY (*Points out front*): That! Off in the distance.

NURSE: They are making way for the exposition.

OLD LADY: What exposition?

NURSE: The International Exposition. They are going to build a tower.

OLD LADY: Another exposition . . .

NURSE: They say it is going to be the tallest structure in the world.

OLD LADY: More foreigners. I am sick of foreigners.

GEORGE: More boats.
          (*An arpeggiated chord. A tugboat appears*)
More trees.
               (*Two chords. More trees track on*)

DOT: George.
               (*Chord*)
Why is it you always get to sit in the shade while I have to stand in the sun?
               (*Chord. No response*)
George?
               (*Still no response*)
Hello, George?
               (*Chord*)
There is someone in this dress!
               (*Twitches slightly, sings to herself*)
A trickle of sweat.
               (*Twitch*)
The back of the —

               (*Twitch*)

21

— head.
He always does this.
> (*Hiss*)

Now the foot is dead.
Sunday in the park with George.
One more Su —
> (*Twitch*)

The collar is damp,
Beginning to pinch.
The bustle's slipping —
> (*Hiss and twitch*)

I won't budge one inch.
> (*Undulating with some pleasure, mixed with tiny twitches of vexation*)

Who was at the zoo, George?
Who was at the zoo?
The monkeys and who, George?
The monkeys and who?

GEORGE: Don't move!

DOT (*Still*):
Artists are bizarre. Fixed. Cold.
That's you, George, you're bizarre. Fixed. Cold.
I like that in a man. Fixed. Cold.
God, it's hot out here.

Well, there are worse things
Than staring at the water on a Sunday.
There are worse things
Than staring at the water
As you're posing for a picture
Being painted by your lover
In the middle of the summer
On an island in the river on a Sunday.
> (GEORGE *races over to* DOT *and rearranges her a bit, as if*

*she were an object, then returns to his easel and resumes
sketching.* DOT *hisses, twitching again)*
The petticoat's wet,
Which adds to the weight.
The sun is blinding.
                    (Closing her eyes)
All right, concentrate . . .

GEORGE: Eyes open, please.

DOT:
Sunday in the park with George . . .

GEORGE: Look out at the water. Not at me.

DOT:
Sunday in the park with George . . .
Concentrate . . . concentrate . . .
          (The dress opens and DOT *walks out of it. The dress closes
          behind her, remaining upright;* GEORGE *continues sketch-
          ing it as if she were still inside. During the following,* DOT
          *moves around the stage, continuing to undulate, taking
          representative poses as punctuation to the music, which is
          heavily rhythmic)*
Well, if you want bread
And respect
And attention,
Not to say connection,
Modelling's no profession.
                    (Does mock poses)
If you want instead,
When you're dead,
Some more public
And more permanent
Expression
                    (Poses)
Of affection,

23

(Poses)

You want a painter,
   (Brief, sharp poses throughout the following)
Poet,
Sculptor, preferably:
Marble, granite, bronze.
Durable.
Something nice with swans
That's durable
Forever.
All it has to be is good.
   (Looking over GEORGE*'s shoulder at his work, then at*
   GEORGE*)*
And George, you're good.
You're really good.

George's stroke is tender,
George's touch is pure.
   (Sits or stands nearby and watches him intently)
Your eyes, George.
I love your eyes, George.
I love your beard, George.
I love your size, George.
But most, George,
Of all,
But most of all,
I love your painting . . .
   (Looking up at the sun)
I think I'm fainting . . .
   *(The dress opens and she steps back into it, resumes pose,
   gives a twitch and a wince, then sings sotto voce again)*
The tip of a stay.
   (Wince)

Right under the tit.
No, don't give in, just
   (Shifts)

24

Lift the arm a bit . . .

GEORGE: Don't lift the arm, please.

DOT:

Sunday in the park with George . . .

GEORGE: The bustle high, please.

DOT:

Not even a nod.
As if I were trees.
The ground could open,
He would still say "please."

Never know with you, George,
Who could know with you?
The others I knew, George.
Before we get through,
I'll get to you, too.

God, I am so hot!

Well, there are worse things
Than staring at the water on a Sunday.
There are worse things
Than staring at the water
As you're posing for a picture
After sleeping on the ferry
After getting up at seven
To come over to an island
In the middle of a river
Half an hour from the city
On a Sunday.
On a Sunday in the park with —

GEORGE (*The music stopping*): Don't move the mouth!!

DOT (*Holds absolutely still for a very long beat. As music resumes, she pours all her extremely mixed emotions into one word*):

— George!
(*Speaks*)
I am getting tired. The sun is too strong today.

GEORGE: Almost finished.

DOT (*Sexy*): I'd rather be in the studio, George.

GEORGE (*Wryly*): I know.

OLD LADY (*Looking across the water*): They are out early today.

NURSE: It is Sunday, Madame.

OLD LADY: That is what I mean, Nurse! Young boys out swimming so early on a Sunday?

NURSE: Well, it is very warm.

OLD LADY: Hand me my parasol.

NURSE: I am, Madame.
(NURSE *stands up and opens the parasol for the* OLD LADY. FRANZ, *a coachman, enters; stares at the two women for a moment, then moves downstage. He sees* GEORGE, *and affects a pose as he sits*)

DOT: Oh, no.

GEORGE: What?

DOT: Look. Look who is over there.

GEORGE: So?

DOT: When he is around, you know who is likely to follow.

GEORGE: You have moved your arm.

DOT: I think they are spying on you, George. I really do.

GEORGE: Are you going to hold your head still?
(*The* NURSE *has wandered over in the vicinity of* FRANZ)

NURSE: You are here awfully early today.

FRANZ (*Speaks with a German accent*): *Ja.* So are you.

NURSE: And working on a Sunday.

FRANZ: *Ja* . . .

NURSE: It is a beautiful day.

FRANZ (*Sexy*): It is too hot.

NURSE: Do you think?

OLD LADY: Where is my fan!

NURSE: I have to go back.

OLD LADY: Nurse, my fan!

NURSE: You did not bring it today, Madame.

OLD LADY: Of course I brought it!

FRANZ: Perhaps we will see each other later.

NURSE: Perhaps . . .

OLD LADY: There it is. Over there.
>   (OLD LADY *picks up the fan*)

NURSE: That is my fan —

OLD LADY: Well, I can use it. Can I not? It was just lying there . . . What is all that commotion?
>   (*Music. Laughter from off right. A wagon tracks on bearing a tableau vivant of Seurat's "Une Baignade Asnières"*)

FRANZ: Jungen! Nicht so laut! Ruhe, bitte!
>   (*The following is heard simultaneously from the characters in the tableau*)

BOY: Yoo-hoo! Dumb and fat!

YOUNG MAN: Hey! Who you staring at?

MAN: Look at the lady with the rear!
>   (*The* YOUNG MAN *gives a loud Bronx cheer*)

27

BOY: Yoo-hoo — kinky beard!

YOUNG MAN: Kinky beard.

YOUNG MAN *and* BOY: Kinky beard!
> (GEORGE *gestures, as when an artist raises and extends his right arm to frame an image before him — all freeze. Silence. A frame comes in around them.* JULES *and* YVONNE, *a well-to-do middle-aged couple, stroll on and pause before the painting*)

JULES: Ahh . . .

YVONNE: Ooh . . .

JULES: Mmm . . .

YVONNE: Oh, dear.

JULES: Oh, my.

YVONNE: Oh, my dear.

JULES (*Sings*):
    It has no presence.

YVONNE (*Sings*):
    No passion.

JULES:
    No life.
>   (*They laugh*)
    It's neither pastoral
    Nor lyrical.

YVONNE (*Giggling*):
    You don't suppose that it's satirical?
>   (*They laugh heartily*)
JULES:
    Just density
    Without intensity —

28

YVONNE:
No life.
                    (*Speaks*)
Boys with their clothes off —

JULES (*Mocking*): *I* must paint a factory next!

YVONNE:
It's so mechanical.

JULES:
Methodical.

YVONNE:
It might be in some dreary
Socialistic periodical.

JULES (*Approvingly*): Good.

YVONNE:
So drab, so cold.

JULES:
And so controlled.

BOTH:
No life.

JULES: His touch is too deliberate, somehow.

YVONNE: The dog.
                    (*They shriek with laughter*)

JULES:
These things get hung —

YVONNE: Hmm.

JULES:
And then they're gone.

YVONNE: Ahhh . . .
Of course he's young —
                    (JULES *shoots her a look. Hastily*)

29

But getting on.

JULES: Oh . . .
All mind, no heart.
No life in his art.

YVONNE:
No life in his *life* —
> (JULES *nods in approval*)

BOTH:
No —
> (*They giggle and chortle*)
Life.
> (*Arpeggio. The* BOYS *in the picture give a loud Bronx cheer. The wagon with the picture tracks off.* JULES *and* YVONNE *turn and slowly stroll upstage.*)

NURSE (*Seeing* JULES): There is that famous artist — what is his name . . .

OLD LADY: What *is* his name?

NURSE: I can never remember their names.
> (JULES *tips his hat to the ladies. The couple continues towards* GEORGE)

JULES: George! Out very early today.
> (GEORGE *nods as he continues sketching.* DOT *turns her back on them*)

GEORGE: Hello, Jules.

YVONNE: A lovely day . . .

JULES: I couldn't be out sketching today — it is too sunny!
> (YVONNE *laughs*)

GEORGE: Have you seen the painting?

JULES: Yes. I was just going to say! Boys bathing — what a curious subject.

We must speak.

YVONNE (*Sincere*): I loved the dog.
>>(*Beat*)

JULES: I *am* pleased there was an independent exhibition.

GEORGE: Yes . . .

JULES: We *must* speak. Really.
>>(*Beat*)

YVONNE: Enjoy the weather.

JULES: Good day.
>>(*As they exit,* YVONNE *stops* JULES *and points to* DOT)

YVONNE: That dress!
>>(*They laugh and exit*)

DOT: I hate them!

GEORGE: Jules is a fine painter.

DOT: I do not care. I hate them.
>>(JULES *and* YVONNE *return*)

JULES: Franz!

YVONNE: We are waiting!
>>(*They exit*)

FRANZ: *Ja*, Madame, Monsieur. At your service.
>>(FRANZ, *who has been hiding behind a tree, eyeing the* NURSE, *quickly dashes offstage after* JULES *and* YVONNE. GEORGE *closes his pad.* DOT *remains frozen*)

GEORGE: Thank you.
>>(*Beat*)

DOT (*Moving*): I began to do it.

GEORGE: What?

31

DOT: Concentrate. Like you said.

GEORGE (*Patronizing*): You did very well.

DOT: Did I really?

GEORGE (*Gathering his belongings*): Yes. I'll meet you back at the studio.

DOT (*Annoyed*): You are not coming?

GEORGE: Not now.
> (*Angry,* DOT *begins to exit*)

Dot. We'll go to the Follies tonight.
> (*She stops, looks at him, then walks off.* GEORGE *walks to the* NURSE *and* OLD LADY)

Bon jour.

NURSE: Bon jour, Monsieur.

GEORGE: Lovely morning, ladies.

NURSE: Yes.

GEORGE: I have my pad and crayons today.

NURSE: Oh, that would —

OLD LADY: Not today!

GEORGE (*Disappointed*): Why not today?

OLD LADY: Too warm.

GEORGE: It *is* warm, but it will not take long. You can go —

OLD LADY (*Continues to look out across the water*): Some other day, Monsieur.
> (*Beat*)

GEORGE (*Kneeling*): It's George, Mother.

OLD LADY (*As if it is to be a secret*): Sssh . . .

GEORGE (*Getting up*): Yes. I guess we will all be back.

(He exits as lights fade to black)

(GEORGE's studio. Downstage, DOT [in a likeness of Seurat's "La Poudreuse"] is at her vanity, powdering her face. Steady, unhurried, persistent rhythmic figure underneath)

DOT *(As she powders rhythmically)*: George taught me all about concentration. "The art of being still," he said.
(Checks herself, then resumes powdering)
I guess I did not learn it soon enough.
(Dips puff in powder)
George likes to be alone.
(Resumes powdering)
Sometimes he will work all night long painting. We fought about that. I need sleep. I love to dream.
(Upstage, GEORGE on a scaffold, behind a large canvas, which is a scrim, comes into view. He is painting. It is an in-progress version of the painting "A Sunday Afternoon on the Island of La Grande Jatte")
George doesn't need as much sleep as everyone else.
(Dips puff, starts powdering neck)
And he never tells me his dreams. George has many secrets.
(Lights down on DOT, up on GEORGE. A number of brushes in his hand, he is covering a section of the canvas — the face of the woman in the foreground — with tiny specks of paint, in the same rhythm as DOT's powdering)

GEORGE *(Pauses, checks)*: Order.
(Dabs with another color, pauses, checks, dabs palette)
Design.
(Dabs with another brush)
Composition.
Tone.
Form.

33

Symmetry.
Balance.
                    (*Sings*)
More red . . .
                    (*Dabs with more intensity*)
And a little more red . . .
                    (*Switches brushes*)
Blue blue blue blue
Blue blue blue blue
Even even . . .
                    (*Switches quickly*)
Good . . .
                    (*Humming*)
Bumbum bum bumbumbum
Bumbum bum . . .
                    (*Paints silently for a moment*)
More red . . .
                    (*Switches brushes again*)
More blue . . .
                    (*Again*)
More beer . . .
    (*Takes a swig from a nearby bottle, always eyeing the canvas, puts the bottle down*)
More light!
    (*He dabs assiduously, delicately attacking the area he is painting*)
Color and light.
There's only color and light.
Yellow and white.
Just blue and yellow and white.
                    (*Addressing the woman he is painting*)
Look at the air, Miss —
                    (*Dabs at the space in front of her*)
See what I mean?
No, look over there, Miss —

34

(Dabs at her eye, pauses, checks it)
That's done with green . . .
(Swirling a brush in the orange cup)
Conjoined with orange . . .
(Lights down on GEORGE, *up on* DOT, *now powdering her
breasts and armpits. Rhythmic figure persists underneath)*

DOT: Nothing seems to fit me right.
(Giggles)
The less I wear, the more comfortable I feel.
(Sings, checking herself)
More rouge . . .
*(Puts puff down, gets rouge, starts applying it in small
rhythmic circles, speaks)*
George is very special. Maybe I'm just not special enough
for him.
(Puts rouge down, picks up eyebrow tweezers, sings)
If my legs were longer.
(Plucks at her eyebrow)
If my bust was smaller.
(Plucks)
If my hands were graceful.
(Plucks)
If my waist was thinner.
(Checks herself)
If my hips were flatter.
(Plucks again)
If my voice was warm.
(Plucks)
If I could concentrate —
(Abruptly, her feet start to can-can under the table)
I'd be in the Follies.
I'd be in a cabaret.
Gentlemen in tall silk hats
And linen spats

35

Would wait with flowers.
I could make them wait for hours.
Giddy young aristocrats
With fancy flats
Who'd drink my health,
And I would be as
Hard as nails . . .
(Looks at her nails, reaches for the buffer)
And they'd only want me more . . .
(Starts buffing nails rhythmically)
If I was a Folly girl . . .
Nah, I wouldn't like it much.
Married men and stupid boys
And too much smoke and all that noise
And all that color and light . . .
(Lights up on GEORGE, talking to the woman in the painting. Rhythmic figure continues underneath)

GEORGE: Aren't you proper today, Miss? Your parasol so properly cocked, your bustle so perfectly upright. No doubt your chin rests at just the proper angle from your chest.
(Addressing the figure of the man next to her)
And you, Sir. Your hat so black. So black to you, perhaps. So red to me.

DOT *(Spraying herself with perfume)*:
None of the others worked at night . . .

GEORGE: So composed for a Sunday.

DOT:
How do you work without the right
(Sprays)
Bright
(Sprays)
White
(Sprays)

36

Light?
                    (*Sprays*)
How do you fathom George?

GEORGE (*Sings in a mutter, trancelike, as he paints*):
    Red red red red
    Red red orange
    Red red orange
    Orange pick up blue
    Pick up red
    Pick up orange
    From the blue-green blue-green
    Blue-green circle
    On the violet diagonal
    Di-ag-ag-ag-ag-ag-o-nal-nal
    Yellow comma yellow comma
            (*Humming, massaging his numb wrist*)
    Numnum num numnumnum
    Numnum num . . .
            (*Sniffs, smelling* DOT*'s perfume*)
    Blue blue blue blue
    Blue still sitting
    Red that perfume
    Blue all night
    Blue-green the window shut
    Dut dut dut
    Dot Dot sitting
    Dot Dot waiting
    Dot Dot getting fat fat fat
    More yellow
    Dot Dot waiting to go
    Out out out but
    No no no George
    Finish the hat finish the hat
    Have to finish the hat first
    Hat hat hat hat

37

Hot hot hot it's hot in here . . .
> (*Whistles a bit, then joyfully*)

Sunday!

Color and light!

DOT (*Pinning up her hair*): But how George looks. He could look forever.

GEORGE:
There's only color and light.

DOT: As if he sees you and he doesn't all at once.

GEORGE:
Purple and white . . .

DOT: What is he thinking when he looks like that?

GEORGE:
. . . And red and purple and white.

DOT: What does he see? Sometimes, not even blinking.

GEORGE (*To the young girls in the painting*):
Look at this glade, girls,
Your cool blue spot.

DOT: His eyes. So dark and shiny.

GEORGE:
No, stay in the shade, girls.
It's getting hot . . .

DOT: Some think cold and black.

GEORGE:
It's getting orange . . .

DOT (*Sings*):
But it's warm inside his eyes . . .

GEORGE (*Dabbing more intensely*):
Hotter . . .

DOT:

And it's soft inside his eyes . . .

(GEORGE *steps around the canvas to get paint or clean a brush. He glances at* DOT. *Their eyes meet for a second, then* DOT *turns back to her mirror*)

And he burns you with his eyes . . .

GEORGE: Look at her looking.

DOT:

And you're studied like the light.

GEORGE: Forever with that mirror. What does she see? The round face, the tiny pout, the soft mouth, the creamy skin . . .

DOT:

And you look inside the eyes.

GEORGE: The pink lips, the red cheeks . . .

DOT:

And you catch him here and there.

GEORGE: The wide eyes. Studying the round face, the tiny pout . . .

DOT:

But he's never really there.

GEORGE: Seeing all the parts and none of the whole.

DOT:

So you want him even more.

GEORGE (*Sings*):

But the way she catches light . . .

DOT:

And you drown inside his eyes . . .

GEORGE:

And the color of her hair . . .

39

DOT:	GEORGE:
I could look at him	I could look at her
Forever . . .	Forever . . .

(*A long beat. Music holds under, gradually fading*)

GEORGE (*At his work table*): It's going well . . .

DOT: Should I wear my red dress or blue?

GEORGE: Red.

(*Beat*)

DOT: Aren't you going to clean up?

GEORGE: Why?

DOT: The Follies, George!

(*Beat*)

GEORGE: I have to finish the hat.

(*He returns to his work.* DOT *slams down her brush and stares at the back of the canvas. She exits. Lights fade downstage as the rhythmic figure resumes. As he paints*)
Damn. The Follies. Will she yell or stay silent? Go without me or sulk in the corner? Will she be in the bed when the hat and the grass and the parasol have finally found their way? . . .

(*Sings*)

Too green . . .
Do I care? . . .
Too blue . . .
Yes . . .
Too soft . . .
What shall I do?

(*Thinks for a moment*)

Well . . .
Red.

(*Continues painting; music swells as he is consumed by light*)

40

(Afternoon. Another Sunday on the island. Downstage right GEORGE *sketches a* BOATMAN; *a cut-out of a black dog stands close by;* NURSE *and* OLD LADY *sit near their tree.* CELESTE #1 *and* CELESTE #2, *young shopgirls, sit on a bench stage left)*

BOATMAN: The water looks different on Sunday.

GEORGE: It is the same water you boat on all week.

BOATMAN (*Contentious*): It looks different from the park.

GEORGE: You prefer watching the boats to the people promenading?

BOATMAN (*Laughing*): People all dressed up in their Sunday-best pretending? Sunday is just another day.
(DOT *and* LOUIS *enter arm in arm. They look out at the water*)
I wear what I always wear — then I don't have to worry.

GEORGE: Worry?

BOATMAN: They leave me alone dressed like this. No one comes near.
(*Music under*)

CELESTE #1: Look who's over there.

CELESTE #2: Dot! Who is she with?

CELESTE #1: Looks like Louis the baker.

CELESTE #2: How did Dot get to be with Louis?

CELESTE #1: She knows how to make dough rise!
(*They laugh*)

NURSE (*Noticing* DOT): There is that woman.

OLD LADY: Who is she with?

NURSE (*Squinting*): Looks like the baker.

OLD LADY: Moving up, I suppose.

41

NURSE: The artist is more handsome.
> (DOT *and* LOUIS *exit*)

OLD LADY: You cannot eat paintings, my dear — not when there's bread in the oven.
> (JULES, YVONNE, *and their child* LOUISE *appear. They stand to one side and strike a pose. Music continues under, slow and stately*)

JULES: They say he is working on an enormous canvas.

YVONNE: I heard somewhere he's painting little specks.

JULES: You heard it from me! A large canvas of specks. Really . . .

YVONNE: Look at him. Drawing a slovenly boatman.

JULES: I think he is trying to play with light.

YVONNE: What next?

JULES: A monkey cage, they say.
> (*They laugh*)

BOATMAN: Sunday hypocrites. That's what they are. Muttering and murmuring about this one and that one. I'll take my old dog for company any day. A dog knows his place. Respects your privacy. Makes no demands.
> (*To the dog*)

Right, Spot?

SPOT (GEORGE): Right.

CELESTE #1 (*Sings*):
They say that George has another woman.

CELESTE #2 (*Sings*):
I'm not surprised.

CELESTE #1:
They say that George only lives with tramps.

CELESTE #2:

I'm not surprised.

CELESTE #1:

They say he prowls through the streets
In his top hat after midnight —

CELESTE #2:

No!

CELESTE #1:

— and stands there staring up at the lamps.

CELESTE #2:

I'm not surprised.

BOTH:

Artists are so crazy . . .

OLD LADY:

Those girls are noisy.

NURSE: Yes, Madame.

OLD LADY (*Referring to* JULES):
That man is famous.

NURSE: Yes, Madame.

OLD LADY (*Referring to* BOATMAN):
That man is filthy.

NURSE: Your son seems to find him interesting.

OLD LADY:

That man's deluded.

                         (NURSE *thinks, nods*)

THE CELESTES:

Artists are so crazy.

OLD LADY *and* NURSE:

Artists are so peculiar.

43

YVONNE: Monkeys!

BOATMAN:
   Overprivileged women
   Complaining,
   Silly little simpering
   Shopgirls,
   Condescending artists
   "Observing,"
   "Perceiving" . . .
   Well, screw them!

ALL:
   Artists are so —

CELESTE #2:
   Crazy.

CELESTE #1:
   Secretive.

BOATMAN:
   High and mighty.

NURSE:
   Interesting.

OLD LADY:
   Unfeeling.

BOATMAN: What do you do with those drawings, anyway?
                    (DOT *and* LOUIS *re-enter*)

DOT (*To* LOUIS): That's George.
             (*All heads turn, first to* DOT, *then to* GEORGE)

JULES: There's a move on to include his work in the next
   group show.

YVONNE: Never!

JULES: I agree.

44

(*Pause*)

I agree.

(*They exit. Music stops*)

CELESTE #1: He draws anyone.

CELESTE #2: Old boatman!

CELESTE #1: Peculiar man.

CELESTE #2: Like his father, I said.

CELESTE #1: I said so first.

> (LOUIS *escorts* DOT *to a park bench stage left and exits.*
> *She sits with a small red lesson book in hand*)

DOT (*Very slowly, she reads aloud*): "Lesson number eight.
Pro-nouns."

> (*Proudly, she repeats the word, looking towards* GEORGE)

Pronouns.

(*She reads*)

"What is a pronoun? A pronoun is the word used in the
place of a noun. Do you recall what a noun is?"

(*Looks up*)

Certainly, I recall.

> (*She pauses, then quickly flips back in the book to the earli-
> er lesson on nouns. She nods her head knowingly, then
> flips back to the present lesson. She reads*)

"Example: Charles has a book. Marie wants Charles' book."

(*To herself*)

Not Marie again . . .

(*Reads*)

"Marie wants *his* book. Fill in the blanks. Charles ran
with Marie's ball. Charles ran with . . ."

(*She writes as she spells aloud*)

h–e–r ball.

(*To herself*)

Get the ball back, Marie.

45

(LOUISE *dashes in upstage*)

OLD LADY: Children should not go unattended.

NURSE: She is very young to be alone.

OLD LADY: I do not like what I see today, Nurse.

NURSE (*Confused*): What do you see?

OLD LADY: Lack of discipline.

NURSE: Oh.

OLD LADY: Not the right direction at all.

BOATMAN: Fools rowing. Call that recreation!

GEORGE: Almost finished.
> (LOUISE *has come up to pet the dog.* BOATMAN *turns on her in a fury*)

BOATMAN: Get away from that dog!
> (*All eyes turn to the* BOATMAN. LOUISE *screams and goes running offstage crying*)

GEORGE: That was hardly necessary!

BOATMAN: How do you know what's necessary? Who are you, with your fancy pad and crayons? You call that work? You smug goddam holier-than-thou shitty little men in your fancy clothes — born with pens and pencils, not pricks! You don't know . . .
> (BOATMAN *storms off.* GEORGE, *stunned, begins to draw the dog*)

CELESTE #1 (*To* GEORGE): Well, what are you going to do — now that you have no one to draw?

CELESTE #2: Sshh. Don't talk to him.

GEORGE: I am drawing this dog.

CELESTE #2: His dog!

46

CELESTE #1: Honestly . . .

GEORGE: I have already sketched you ladies.

CELESTE #1: What!

CELESTE #2: You have?
(*The* CELESTES *approach* GEORGE)

CELESTE #1: I do not believe you.

CELESTE #2: When?
(*During the above, the* OLD LADY *and* NURSE *have exited*)

GEORGE: A few Sundays ago.

CELESTE #1: But we never sat for you.

GEORGE: I studied you from afar.

CELESTE #2: No!

CELESTE #1: Where were you?

CELESTE #2: I want to see.

GEORGE: Some day you shall.

THE CELESTES: When?

GEORGE: Good day.
(GEORGE *moves upstage*)

CELESTE #1: He did not so much as ask.

CELESTE #2: No respect for a person's privacy.

CELESTE #1: I would not sit for him anyway.

CELESTE #2: Probably that's why he did not ask.
(*They exit*)

GEORGE (*From across the stage to* DOT): Good afternoon.

DOT (*Surprised*): Hello.

GEORGE: Lesson number eight?

47

DOT: Yes. Pronouns. My writing is improving. I even keep notes in the back of the book.

GEORGE: Good for you.

DOT: How is your painting coming along?

GEORGE: Slowly.

DOT: Are you getting more work done now that you have fewer distractions in the studio?

GEORGE (*Beat; he moves closer*): It has been quiet there.
    (LOUIS *bounds onstage with a pastry tin*)

LOUIS: Dot. I made your favorite —
    (*He stops when he sees* GEORGE)

GEORGE: Good day.
    (*He retreats across the stage.* DOT *watches him, then turns to* LOUIS)

LOUIS (*Opens the tin*): Creampuffs!
    (*The bench on which they are sitting tracks offstage as* DOT *continues to look at* GEORGE. GEORGE, *who has been staring at his sketch of* SPOT, *looks over and sees they have left. Music. He begins to lose himself in his work. Lights change, leaving the dog onstage.* GEORGE *sketches the dog*)

GEORGE (*Sings*):
If the head was smaller.
If the tail were longer.
If he faced the water.
If the paws were hidden.
If the neck was darker.
If the back was curved.
More like the parasol.

Bumbum bum bumbumbum
Bumbum bum . . .

More shade.
More tail.

More grass . . .
Would you like some more grass?
Mmmm . . .

SPOT (GEORGE) (*Barks*):
Ruff! Ruff!
Thanks, the week has been
                    (*Barks*)
Rough!
When you're stuck for life on a garbage scow —
                    (*Sniffs around*)
Only forty feet long from stern to prow,
And a crackpot in the bow — wow, rough!
                    (*Sniffs*)
The planks are rough
And the wind is rough
And the master's drunk and mean and —
                    (*Sniffs*)
Grrrruff! Gruff!
With the fish and scum
And planks and ballast,
                    (*Sniffs*)
The nose gets numb
And the paws get calloused.
And with splinters in your ass,
You look forward to the grass
On Sunday.
The day off.
                    (*Barks*)
Off! Off! Off!
Off!

The grass needs to be thicker. Perhaps a few weeds. With
some ants, if you would. I love fresh ants.

49

Roaming around on Sunday,
Poking among the roots and rocks.
Nose to the ground on Sunday,
Studying all the shoes and socks.
Everything's worth it Sunday,
The day off.

> (*Sniffs*)

Bits of pastry.

> (*Sniffs*)

Piece of chicken.

> (*Sniffs*)

Here's a handkerchief
That somebody was sick in.

> (*Sniffs*)

There's a thistle.

> (*Sniffs*)

That's a shallot.

> (*Sniffs*)

That's a dripping
From the loony with the palette.

> (*A cut-out of a pug dog,* FIFI, *appears*)

FIFI (GEORGE):
Yap! Yap!

> (*Pants*)

Yap!

> (*High voice*)

Out for the day on Sunday,
Off of my lady's lap at last.
Yapping away on Sunday
Helps you forget the week just past —

> (*Yelps*)

Yep! Yep!
Everything's worth it Sunday,
The day off.
Yep!

Stuck all week on a lady's lap,
Nothing to do but yawn and nap,
Can you blame me if I yap?

SPOT:
  Nope.

FIFI: There's just so much attention a dog can take.
  Being alone on Sunday,
  Rolling around in mud and dirt —

SPOT:
  Begging a bone on Sunday,
  Settling for a spoiled dessert —

FIFI:
  Everything's worth it

SPOT:
  Sunday —

FIFI:
  The day off.

SPOT (*Sniffs*):
  Something fuzzy.

FIFI (*Sniffs*):
  Something furry.

SPOT (*Sniffs*):
  Something pink
  That someone tore off in a hurry.

FIFI:
  What's the muddle
  In the middle?

SPOT:
  That's the puddle
  Where the poodle did the piddle.

51

(Cut-out of HORN PLAYER *rises from the stage. Two horn calls. Music continues under. Enter* FRANZ; FRIEDA, *his wife; the* CELESTES, *with fishing poles; and* NURSE*)*

GEORGE *(Sings)*:
Taking the day on Sunday,
Now that the dreary week is dead.
Getting away on Sunday
Brightens the dreary week ahead.
Everyone's on display on Sunday —

ALL:
The day off!
*(*GEORGE *flips open a page of his sketchbook and starts to sketch the* NURSE *as she clucks at the ducks)*

GEORGE:
Bonnet flapping,
Bustle sliding,
Like a rocking horse that nobody's been riding.
There's a daisy —
And some clover —
And that interesting fellow looking over . . .

OLD LADY *(Offstage)*: Nurse!

NURSE *and* GEORGE *(Sing)*:
One day is much like any other,
Listening to her snap and drone.

NURSE:
Still, Sunday with someone's dotty mother
Is better than Sunday with your own.
Mothers may drone, mothers may whine —
Tending to his, though, is perfectly fine.
It pays for the nurse that is tending to mine
On Sunday,
My day off.
(The CELESTES, *fishing. Music continues under)*

52

CELESTE #2: This is just ridiculous.

CELESTE #1: Why shouldn't we fish?

CELESTE #2: No one will notice us anyway.
(SOLDIER *enters, attached to a life-size cut-out of another soldier, his* COMPANION)

CELESTE #1: Look.

CELESTE #2: Where?

CELESTE #1: Soldiers.

CELESTE #2: Alone.

CELESTE #1: What did I tell you?

CELESTE #2: They'll never talk to us if we fish. Why don't we —

CELESTE #1: It's a beautiful day for fishing.
(*She smiles in the direction of the* SOLDIERS)

SOLDIER (*Looking to his* COMPANION): What do you think?
(*Beat*)
I like the one in the light hat.
(LOUISE *enters, notices* FRIEDA *and* FRANZ, *and dashes over to them*)

LOUISE: Frieda, Frieda —

FRANZ: Oh, no.

FRIEDA (*Speaks with a German accent*): Not now, Louise.

LOUISE: I want to play.

FRANZ: Go away, Louise. We are not working today.

LOUISE: Let's go throw stones at the ducks.

FRIEDA: Louise! Do not throw stones at the ducks!

LOUISE: Why not?

FRANZ: You know why not, and you know this is our day off,

53

so go find your mother and throw some stones at her, why don't you.

(*He begins to choke* LOUISE; FRIEDA *releases his grip*)

FRIEDA: Franz!

LOUISE: I'm telling.

FRANZ: Good. Go!

(LOUISE *exits*)

FRIEDA: Franzel — relax.

FRANZ: *Ja* . . . relax.
(*He opens a bottle of wine.* GEORGE *flips a page and starts to sketch* FRANZ *and* FRIEDA)

GEORGE *and* FRIEDA (*Sing*):
Second bottle . . .

GEORGE *and* FRANZ (*As* FRANZ *looks off at* NURSE):
Ah, she looks for me . . .

FRIEDA:
He is bursting to go . . .

FRANZ:
Near the fountain . . .

FRIEDA:
I could let him . . .

FRANZ:
How to manage it — ?

FRIEDA:
No.

(*Speaks*)
You know, Franz — I believe that artist is drawing us.

FRANZ: Who?

FRIEDA: Monsieur's friend.

FRANZ (*Sees* GEORGE. *They pose*): Monsieur would never think to draw us! We are only people he looks down upon.
(*Pause*)
I should have been an artist. I was never intended for work.

FRIEDA: Artists work, Franz. I believe they work very hard.

FRANZ: Work! . . . *We* work.
(*Sings*)
We serve their food,
We carve their meat,
We tend to their house,
We polish their
Silverware.

FRIEDA:
The food we serve
We also eat.

FRANZ:
For them we rush,
Wash and brush,
Wipe and wax —

FRIEDA:
Franz, relax.

FRANZ:
While he "creates,"
We scrape their plates
And dust their knickknacks,
Hundreds to the shelf.
Work is what you do for others,
Liebchen,
Art is what you do for yourself.
(JULES *enters, as if looking for someone. Notices* GEORGE *instead*)

JULES: Working on Sunday again? You should give yourself a day off.

55

GEORGE: Why?

JULES: You must need time to replenish — or does your well never run dry?
> (*Laughs; notices* FRIEDA *and* FRANZ)

Drawing my servants? Certainly, George, you could find more colorful subjects.

GEORGE: Who should I be sketching?

JULES: How about that pretty friend of yours. Now why did I see her arm-in-arm with the baker today?
> (GEORGE *looks up*)

She is a pretty subject.

GEORGE: Yes . . .
> (BOATMAN *enters*)

JULES: Your life needs spice, George. Go to some parties. That is where you'll meet prospective buyers. Have some fun. The work is bound to reflect —

GEORGE: You don't like my work, do you?

JULES: I did once.

GEORGE: You find it too tight.

JULES: People are talking about your work. You have your admirers, but you —

GEORGE: I am using a different brushstroke.

JULES (*Getting angry*): Always changing! Why keep changing?

GEORGE: Because I do not paint for your approval.
> (*Beat*)

JULES: And I suppose that is why I like you.
> (*Begins to walk away*)

Good to see you, George.

(JULES *crosses as if to exit*)

GEORGE (*Calling after him*): Jules! I would like you to come to the studio some time. See the new work . . .

JULES: For my approval?

GEORGE: No! For your opinion.

JULES (*Considers the offer*): Very well.
  (*He exits.* GEORGE *flips a page over and starts sketching the* BOATMAN)

GEORGE *and* BOATMAN (*Sing*):
  You and me, pal,
  We're the loonies.
  Did you know that?
  Bet you didn't know that.

BOATMAN:
  'Cause we tell them the truth!

  Who you drawing?
  Who the hell you think you're drawing?
  Me?
  You don't know me!
  Go on drawing,
  Since you're drawing only what you want to see,
  Anyway!
          (*Points to his eyepatch*)
  One eye, no illusion —
  That you get with two:
          (*Points to* GEORGE's *eye*)
  One for what is true.
          (*Points to the other*)
  One for what suits you.
  Draw your wrong conclusion,
  All you artists do.
  I see what is true . . .

57

(*Music continues under*)
Sitting there, looking everyone up and down. Studying every move like *you* see something different, like your eyes know more —
(*Sings*)
You and me, pal,
We're society's fault.
(YVONNE, LOUISE, OLD LADY *enter.* GEORGE *packs up his belongings*)

ALL (*Sing*):
Taking the day on Sunday
After another week is dead.

OLD LADY: Nurse!

ALL:
Getting away on Sunday
Brightens the dreary week ahead.

OLD LADY: Nurse!
(GEORGE *begins to exit, crossing paths with* DOT *and* LOUIS, *who enter. He gives* DOT *a hasty tip-of-the-hat and makes a speedy exit*)

ALL:
Leaving the city pressure
Behind you,
Off where the air is fresher,
Where green, blue,
Blind you —
(LOUIS *leaves* DOT *to offer some pastries to his friends in the park. Throughout the song, he divides his time between* DOT *and the others*)

DOT (*Looking offstage in the direction of* GEORGE *'s exit, sings*):
Hello, George . . .
Where did you go, George?
I know you're near, George.

58

I caught your eyes, George.
I want your ear, George.
I've a surprise, George . . .

Everybody loves Louis,
Louis' simple and kind.
Everybody loves Louis,
Louis' lovable.

FRANZ (*Greeting* LOUIS): Louis!

DOT:
Seems we never know, do we,
Who we're going to find?
                    (*Tenderly*)
And Louis the baker —
Is not what I had in mind.
But . . .

Louis' really an artist:
Louis' cakes are an art.
Louis isn't the smartest —
Louis' popular.
Everybody loves Louis:
Louis bakes from the heart . . .

The bread, George.
I mean the bread, George.
And then in bed, George . . .
I mean he kneads me —
I mean like dough, George . . .
Hello, George . . .

Louis' always so pleasant,
Louis' always so fair.
Louis makes you feel present,
Louis' generous.
That's the thing about Louis:

Louis always is "there."
Louis' thoughts are not hard to follow,
Louis' art is not hard to swallow.

Not that Louis' perfection —
That's what makes him ideal.
Hardly anything worth objection:
Louis drinks a bit,
Louis blinks a bit.
Louis makes a connection,
That's the thing that you feel . . .

We lose things.
And then we choose things.
And there are Louis's
And there are Georges —
Well, Louis's
And George.

But George has George
And I need —
Someone —
Louis — !
         (LOUIS *gives her a pastry and exits*)
Everybody loves Louis,
Him as well as his cakes.
Everybody loves Louis,
Me included, George.
Not afraid to be gooey,
Louis sells what he makes.
Everybody gets along with him.
That's the trouble, nothing's wrong with him.

Louis has to bake his way,
George can only bake his . . .
         (*Licks a pastry*)
Louis it is!

(*She throws pastry away and exits. Enter an American southern couple,* MR. *and* MRS., *followed by* GEORGE, *who sketches them. They are overdressed, eating French pastries and studying the people in the park*)

MR.: Paris looks nothin' like the paintings.

MRS.: I know.

MR. (*Looking about*): I don't see any passion, do you?

MRS.: None.

MR.: The French are so placid.

MRS.: I don't think they have much style, either.

MR.: What's all the carryin' on back home? Delicious pastries, though.

MRS.: Excellent.

MR.: Lookin' at those boats over there makes me think of our return voyage.

MRS.: I long to be back home.

MR.: You do?

MRS.: How soon could we leave?

MR.: You're that anxious to leave? But, Peaches, we just arrived!

MRS.: I know!

MR. (*Gives it a moment's thought*): I don't like it here either! We'll go right back to the hotel and I'll book passage for the end of the week. We'll go to the galleries this afternoon and then we'll be on our way home!

MRS.: I am so relieved.
(*As they exit*)
I *will* miss these pastries, though.

61

MR.: We'll take a baker with us, too.

MRS.: Wonderful!

(*They exit*)

CELESTE #1: You really should try using that pole.

CELESTE #2: It won't make any difference.

CELESTE #1 (*Starts yelping as if she had caught a fish*): Oh! Oh!

CELESTE #2: What is wrong?

CELESTE #1: Just sit there.
(*She carries on some more, looking in the direction of the* SOLDIER *and his* COMPANION, *who converse for a moment, then come over*)

SOLDIER: May we be of some service, Madame?

CELESTE #1: Mademoiselle.

CELESTE #2: She has a fish.

CELESTE #1: He knows.

SOLDIER: Allow me.
(SOLDIER *takes the pole from her and pulls in the line and hook. There is nothing on the end*)

CELESTE #1: Oh. It tugged so . . .

SOLDIER: There's no sign of a fish here.

CELESTE #1: Oh me. My name is Celeste. This is my friend.

CELESTE #2: Celeste.
(SOLDIER *fools with fishing pole*)

CELESTE #1: Do you have a name?

SOLDIER: I beg your pardon. Napoleon. Some people feel I should change it.
(*The* CELESTES *shake their heads no*)

CELESTE #2: And your friend?

SOLDIER: Yes. He is my friend.

CELESTE #1 (*Giggling, to* SOLDIER): He's very quiet.

SOLDIER: Yes. Actually he is. He lost his hearing during combat exercises.

CELESTE #1: What a shame.

SOLDIER: He can't speak, either.

CELESTE #2: Oh. How dreadful.

SOLDIER: We have become very close, though.

CELESTE #1 (*Nervous*): So I see.
(Music)

SOLDIER *and* GEORGE (*Sudden and loud, sing*):
Mademoiselles,
I and my friend,
We are but soldiers!
>(*Rumble from the* COMPANION: SOLDIER *raises hand to quiet him*)

SOLDIER:
Passing the time
In between wars
For weeks at an end.

CELESTE #1 (*Aside*):
Both of them are perfect.

CELESTE #2:
You can have the other.

CELESTE #1:
I don't want the other.

CELESTE #2:
I don't want the other either.

SOLDIER:

And after a week
Spent mostly indoors
With nothing but soldiers,
Ladies, I and my friend
Trust we will not offend,
Which we'd never intend,
By suggesting we spend —

THE CELESTES (*Excited*):

Oh, spend —

SOLDIER:

— this magnificent Sunday —

THE CELESTES (*A bit deflated*):

Oh, Sunday —

SOLDIER:

— with you and your friend.
(SOLDIER *offers his arm. Both* CELESTES *rush to take it;* CELESTE #1 *gets there first.* CELESTE #2 *tries to get in between the* SOLDIERS, *can't, and rather than join the* COMPANION, *takes the arm of* CELESTE #1. *They all start to promenade*)

CELESTE #2 (*To* CELESTE #1):

The one on the right's an awful bore . . .

CELESTE #1:

He's been in a war.

SOLDIER (*To* COMPANION):

We may get a meal and we might get more . . .
(CELESTE #1 *shakes free of* CELESTE #2, *grabs the arm of the* SOLDIER, *freeing him from his* COMPANION)

CELESTE #1 *and* SOLDIER (*To themselves, as they exit*):

It's certainly fine for Sunday . . .

It's certainly fine for Sunday . . .
>> (*Dejected,* CELESTE #2 *grabs the* COMPANION)

CELESTE #2 (*As she exits, carrying* COMPANION):
It's certainly fine for Sunday . . .
>> (GEORGE *is alone. He moves downstage as* FIFI *rises. He sits*)

GEORGE (*Leafing back through his sketches. Sings*):
Mademoiselles . . .
>> (*Flips a page*)

You and me, pal . . .
>> (*Flips*)

Second bottle . . .
Ah, she looks for me . . .
>> (*Flips*)

Bonnet flapping . . .
>> (*Flips*)

Yapping . . .
>> (*Flips*)

Ruff! . . .
Chicken . . .
Pastry . . .
>> (*Licks lip; looks offstage to where* DOT *has exited*)

Yes, she looks for me — good.
Let her look for me to tell me why she left me —
As I always knew she would.
I had thought she understood.
They have never understood.
And no reason that they should.
But if anybody could . . .

Finishing the hat,
How you have to finish the hat.
How you watch the rest of the world
From a window
While you finish the hat.

65

Mapping out a sky,
What you feel like, planning a sky,
What you feel when voices that come
Through the window
Go
Until they distance and die,
Until there's nothing but sky.

And how you're always turning back too late
From the grass or the stick
Or the dog or the light,
How the kind of woman willing to wait's
Not the kind that you want to find waiting
To return you to the night,
Dizzy from the height,
Coming from the hat,
Studying the hat,
Entering the world of the hat,
Reaching through the world of the hat
Like a window,
Back to this one from that.

Studying a face,
Stepping back to look at a face
Leaves a little space in the way like a window,
But to see —
It's the only way to see.

And when the woman that you wanted goes,
You can say to yourself, "Well, I give what I give."
But the woman who won't wait for you knows
That, however you live,
There's a part of you always standing by,
Mapping out the sky,
Finishing a hat . . .
Starting on a hat . . .
Finishing a hat . . .

(Showing sketch to FIFI)

Look, I made a hat . . .

Where there never was a hat . . .

(MR. *and* MRS. *enter stage right. They are lost. The* BOAT-MAN *crosses near them and they stop him in his path)*

MR.: Excusez, Masseur. We are lost.

BOATMAN: Huh?

MRS.: Let me try, Daddy.

(Slowly and wildly gesticulating with her every word)

We are alien here. Unable to find passage off island.

BOATMAN *(Pointing to the water)*: Why don't you just walk into the water until your lungs fill up and you die.

(BOATMAN *crosses away from them, laughing)*

MRS.: I detest these people.

MR. *(Spotting* LOUIS, *who has entered in search of* DOT): Isn't that the baker?

MRS.: Why, yes it is!

(They cross to LOUIS. GEORGE *brings on the* HORN PLAYER *cut-out.* OLD LADY *enters)*

OLD LADY: Where is that tree? Nurse? NURSE!

(Horn call. DOT *enters, and suddenly she and* GEORGE *are still, staring at one another. Everyone onstage turns slowly to them. People begin to sing fragments of songs.* DOT *and* GEORGE *move closer to one another, circling each other like gun duellers. The others close in around them until* DOT *and* GEORGE *stop, opposite each other. Silence.* DOT *takes her bustle and defiantly turns it around, creating a pregnant stance. There is an audible gasp from the onlookers. Blackout)*

(Music. Lights slowly come up on GEORGE *in his studio, painting.* DOT *enters and joins* GEORGE *behind the paint-*

67

*ing. He continues painting as she watches. He stops for a
moment when he sees her, then continues working)*

DOT: You are almost finished.

GEORGE: If I do not change my mind again. And you?

DOT: Two more months.

GEORGE: You cannot change your mind.

DOT: Nor do I want to.
> (*Beat*)
Is it going to be exhibited?

GEORGE: I am not sure. Jules is coming over to look at it.
Any minute, in fact.

DOT: Oh, I hope you don't mind my coming.

GEORGE: What is it that you want, Dot?

DOT: George. I would like my painting.

GEORGE: Your painting?

DOT: The one of me powdering.

GEORGE: I did not know that it was yours.

DOT: You said once that I could have it.

GEORGE: In my sleep?

DOT: I want something to remember you by.

GEORGE: You don't have enough now?

DOT: I want the painting, too.
> (GEORGE *stops painting*)

GEORGE: I understand you and Louis are getting married.

DOT: Yes.

GEORGE: He must love you very much to take you in that
condition.

DOT: He does.

GEORGE: I didn't think you would go through with it. I did not think that was what you really wanted.

DOT: I don't think I can have what I really want. Louis is what I think I need.

GEORGE: Yes. Louis will take you to the Follies! Correct?

DOT: George, I didn't come here to argue.
(JULES *and* YVONNE *enter*)

JULES: George?

GEORGE: Back here, Jules.

DOT: I will go.

GEORGE: Don't leave! It will only be a minute —

JULES (*Crossing behind canvas to* GEORGE): There you are. I brought Yvonne along.

YVONNE: May I take a peek?

DOT: I will wait in the other room.

YVONNE (*Sees* DOT): I hope we are not interrupting you.
(*She and* JULES *step back and study the painting.* GEORGE *looks at* DOT *as she exits to the front room*)

JULES: It is so large. How can you get any perspective? And this light . . .
(GEORGE *pulls a lantern close to the canvas*)

GEORGE: Stand here.

YVONNE: Extraordinary! Excuse me.
(YVONNE *exits into the other room.* DOT *is sitting at her vanity, which is now cleared of her belongings.* YVONNE *and* DOT *look at each other for a moment*)
Talk of painting bores me. It is hard to escape it when you are with an artist.

69

(*Beat*)

I do not know how you can walk up all those steps in your condition. I remember when I had Louise. I could never be on my feet for long periods of time. Certainly could never navigate steps.

DOT: Did someone carry you around?

YVONNE: Why are you so cool to me?

DOT: Maybe I don't like you.

YVONNE: Whatever have I done to make you feel that way?

DOT: "Whatever have I done . . . ?" Maybe it is the way you speak. What are you really doing here?

YVONNE: You know why we are here. So Jules can look at George's work.

DOT: I do not understand why George invites you. He knows you do not like his painting.

YVONNE: That is not entirely true. Jules has great respect for George. And he has encouraged him since they were in school.

DOT: That is not what I hear. Jules is jealous of George now.

YVONNE (*Beat*): Well . . . jealousy is a form of flattery, is it not? I have been jealous of you on occasion.
    (DOT *looks surprised*)
When I have seen George drawing you in the park. Jules has rarely sketched me.

DOT: You are his wife.

YVONNE (*Uncomfortable*): Too flat. Too angular.

DOT: Modeling is hard work. You wouldn't like it anyway.

YVONNE: It is worth it, don't you think?

DOT: Sometimes . . .

70

YVONNE: Has your life changed much now that you are with the baker?

DOT: I suppose. He enjoys caring for me.

YVONNE: You are very lucky. Oh, I suppose Jules cares — but there are times when he just does not know Louise and I are there. George always seems so oblivious to everyone.
(*Lowers her voice*)
Jules says that is what is wrong with his painting. Too obsessive. You have to have a life! Don't you agree?
(DOT *nods*)

JULES: George . . . I do not know what to say. What *is* this?

GEORGE: What is the dominant color? The flower on the hat?

JULES: Is this a school exam, George?

GEORGE: What is that color?

JULES (*Bored*): Violet.
(GEORGE *takes him by the hand and moves him closer to the canvas*)

GEORGE: See? Red and blue. Your eye made the violet.

JULES: So?

GEORGE: So, your eye is perceiving both red and blue *and* violet. Only eleven colors — no black — divided, not mixed on the palette, mixed by the eye. Can't you see the shimmering?

JULES: George . . .

GEORGE: Science, Jules. Fixed laws for color, like music.

JULES: You are a painter, not a scientist! You cannot even see these faces!

GEORGE: I am not painting faces! I am —

JULES: George! I have touted your work in the past, and now

71

you are embarrassing me! People are talking —

GEORGE: Why should I paint like you or anybody else? I am trying to get through to something new. Something that is my own.

JULES: And I am trying to understand.

GEORGE: And I want you to understand. Look at the canvas, Jules. Really look at it.

JULES: George! Let us get to the point. You have invited me here because you want me to try to get this included in the next group show.

GEORGE (*Beat — embarrassed*): It will be finished soon. I want it to be seen.
(YVONNE, *who has been eavesdropping at the studio door, leans into the room*)

YVONNE: Jules, I am sorry to interrupt, but we really must be going. You know we have an engagement.

JULES: Yes.

YVONNE: Thank you, George.

JULES: Yes. Thank you.

GEORGE: Yes. Thank you for coming.

JULES: I will give the matter some thought.
(*They exit.* GEORGE *stands motionless for a moment staring at the canvas, then dives into his work, painting the girls*)

GEORGE: He does not like you. He does not understand or appreciate you. He can only see you as everyone else does. Afraid to take you apart and put you back together again for himself. But we will not let anyone deter us, will we?
(*Hums*)
Bumbum bum bumbumbum bumbum —

DOT (*Calling to him*): George!

(GEORGE, *embarrassed, crosses in front of canvas. He begins to speak.* DOT *tries to interrupt him*)

GEORGE:
Excuse me — speaking with Jules about the painting — well, I just picked up my brushes — I do not believe he even looked at the painting, though —

DOT:
You asked me to stay, George, and then you forget that I am even here. George!

DOT: I have something to tell you.

GEORGE: Yes. Now, about "your" painting —

DOT: I may be going away.

(*Beat*)

To America.

GEORGE: Alone.

DOT: Of course not! With Louis. He has work.

GEORGE: When?

DOT: After the baby arrives.

GEORGE: You will not like it there.

DOT: How do you know?

GEORGE (*Getting angry*): I have read about America. Why are you telling me this? First, you ask for a painting that is *not* yours — then you tell me this.

(*Beginning to return to the studio*)

I have work to do.

(*Chord; music continues under*)

DOT: Yes, George, run to your work. Hide behind your painting. I have come to tell you I am leaving because I thought you might *care* to know — foolish of me, because you care about nothing —

73

GEORGE: I care about many things —

DOT: Things — not people.

GEORGE: People, too. I cannot divide my feelings up as neatly as you, and I am not hiding behind my canvas — I am living in it.

DOT (*Sings*):
What you care for is yourself.

GEORGE: I care about this painting. *You* will be in this painting.

DOT:
I am something you can use.

GEORGE (*Sings*):
I had thought you understood.

DOT:
It's because I understand that I left,
That I am leaving.

GEORGE:
Then there's nothing I can say,
Is there?

DOT:
Yes, George, there is!

You could tell me not to go.
Say it to me,
Tell me not to go.
Tell me that you're hurt,
Tell me you're relieved,
Tell me that you're bored —
Anything, but don't assume I know.
Tell me what you feel!

GEORGE:
What I feel?
You know exactly how I feel.

Why do you insist
You must hear the words,
When you know I cannot give you words?
Not the ones you need.

There's nothing to say.
I cannot be what you want.

DOT:

What do *you* want, George?

GEORGE:

I needed you and you left.

DOT:

There was no room for me —

GEORGE (*Overriding her*):

You will not accept who I am.
I am what I do —
Which you knew,
Which you always knew,
Which I thought you were a part of!
                    (*He goes behind the canvas*)

DOT:

No,
You are complete, George,
You are your own.
We do not belong together.
You are complete, George,
You are alone.
I am unfinished,
I am diminished
With or without you.

We do not belong together,
And we should have belonged together.
What made it so right together

Is what made it all wrong.

No one is you, George,
There we agree,
But others will do, George.
No one is you and
No one can be,
But no one is me, George,
No one is me.
We do not belong together.
And we'll never belong — !

You have a mission,
A mission to see.
Now I have one too, George.
And we should have belonged together.

I have to move on.
> (DOT *leaves.* GEORGE *stops painting and comes from around the canvas. He is left standing alone onstage. The lights fade*)

> (*The set changes back to the park scene around him. When the change is complete, he moves downstage right with the* OLD LADY, *and begins to draw her. They are alone, except for the cut-out of the* COMPANION, *which stands towards the rear of the stage. There is a change of tone in both* GEORGE *and the* OLD LADY. *She has assumed a kind of loving attitude, soft and dreamlike.* GEORGE *is rather sullen in her presence*)

OLD LADY (*Staring across the water*): I remember when you were a little boy. You would rise up early on a Sunday morning and go for a swim . . .

GEORGE: I do not know how to swim.

OLD LADY: The boys would come by the house to get you . . .

GEORGE: I have always been petrified of the water.

76

OLD LADY: And your father would walk you all to the banks of the Seine . . .

GEORGE: Father was never faithful to us.

OLD LADY: And he would give you boys careful instruction, telling you just how far to swim out . . .

GEORGE: And he certainly never instructed.

OLD LADY: And now, look across there — in the distance — all those beautiful trees cut down for a foolish tower.
(*Music under*)

GEORGE: I do not think there were ever trees there.

OLD LADY: How I loved the view from here . . .
(*Sings*)
Changing . . .

GEORGE: I am quite certain that was an open field . . .

OLD LADY:
It keeps changing.

GEORGE: I used to play there as a child.

OLD LADY:
I see towers
Where there were trees.

Going,
All the stillness,
The solitude,
Georgie.

Sundays,
Disappearing
All the time,
When things were beautiful . . .

GEORGE (*Sings*):
All things are beautiful,

77

Mother.
All trees, all towers,
Beautiful.
That tower —
Beautiful, Mother,
See?

(*Gestures*)

A perfect tree.

Pretty isn't beautiful, Mother,
Pretty is what changes.
What the eye arranges
Is what is beautiful.

OLD LADY:
Fading . . .

GEORGE:
I'm changing.
You're changing.

OLD LADY:
It keeps fading . . .

GEORGE:
I'll draw us now before we fade, Mother.

OLD LADY:
It keeps melting
Before our eyes.

GEORGE:
You watch
While I revise the world.

OLD LADY:
Changing,
As we sit here —
Quick, draw it all,
Georgie!

78

OLD LADY *and* GEORGE:
Sundays —

OLD LADY:
Disappearing,
As we look —

GEORGE: Look! . . . Look! . . .

OLD LADY (*Not listening, fondly*):
You make it beautiful.
                    (*Music continues*)
Oh, Georgie, how I long for the old view.
    (*Music stops. The* SOLDIER *and* CELESTE #2 *enter arm-in-
    arm and promenade*)

SOLDIER (*Noticing his* COMPANION): I am glad to be free of him.

CELESTE #2: Friends can be confining.

SOLDIER: He never understood my moods.

CELESTE #2: She only thought of herself.
    (MR. *and* MRS. *enter. He is carrying a big steamer trunk.
    She is carrying a number of famous paintings, framed,
    under her arm. They are followed by* DOT, *who is carrying
    her baby bundled in white, and* LOUIS)

SOLDIER:
It felt as if I had this
burden at my side.

CELESTE #2:
She never really cared
about me.

SOLDIER:
We had very different
tastes.

MR.:
This damned island again!
I do not understand why we
are not goin' straight to
our boat.

MRS.:
They wanted to come here
first.

CELESTE #2:
She had no taste.

SOLDIER:
She did seem rather pushy.

CELESTE #2:
Very! And he was so odd.

SOLDIER:
(*Angry*)
HE IS NOT ODD!

MR.:
That much I figured out — but why? Didn't you ask them?

MRS.:
I don't know.

(MR. *and* MRS. *are stopped by the* SOLDIER*'s line, "He is not odd"*)

CELESTE #2: No. No, I didn't really mean odd . . .
    (*They exit.* LOUISE *runs onstage.* BOATMAN *rushes after her*)

BOATMAN (*Mutters as he chases after* LOUISE): . . . you better not let me get my hands on you, you little toad.
    (LOUISE *puts her hand over her eye and stiffens her leg in imitation of the* BOATMAN. *As he chases her offstage*)
Now stop that!

MR.: Are we ever going to get home?!
    (MR. *and* MRS. *exit.* DOT *crosses downstage to* GEORGE)

GEORGE (*Not looking up*): You are blocking my light.

DOT: Marie and I came to watch.

GEORGE (*Turning towards* DOT): Marie . . .
    (*Back to his sketch pad*)
You know I do not like anyone staring over my shoulder.

DOT: Yes, I know.
    (*She moves to another position*)
George, we are about to leave for America. I have come to ask for the painting of me powdering again. I would like to take it with me.

GEORGE (*He stops for a moment*): Oh? I have repainted it.
(*He draws*)

DOT: What?

GEORGE: Another model.

DOT: You knew I wanted it.

GEORGE: Perhaps if you had remained still —

DOT: Perhaps if you would look up from your pad! What is wrong with you, George? Can you not even look at your own child?

GEORGE: She is not my child. Louis is her father.

DOT: Louis is not her father.

GEORGE: Louis is her father now. Louis will be a loving and attentive father. I cannot because I cannot look up from my pad.
(*She stands speechless for a moment, then begins to walk away;* GEORGE *turns to her*)
Dot.
(*She stops*)
I *am* sorry.
(DOT *and* LOUIS *exit.* GEORGE *drawing* OLD LADY)

OLD LADY: I worry about you, George.

GEORGE: Could you turn slightly toward me, please.
(*She does so*)

OLD LADY: No future in dreaming.

GEORGE: Drop the head a little, please.
(*She does so.* CELESTE #1 *enters and goes to the* COMPANION)

OLD LADY: I worry about you and that woman, too.

GEORGE: I have another woman in my life now.

OLD LADY: They are all the same woman.

81

GEORGE (*Chuckles*): Variations on a theme.

OLD LADY: Ah, you always drifted as a child.

GEORGE (*Muttering*): Shadows are too heavy.

OLD LADY: You were always in some other place — seeing something no one else could see.

GEORGE: Softer light.
> (*Lights dim slowly*)

OLD LADY: We tried to get through to you, George. Really we did.
> (GEORGE *stops drawing. He looks at her. Looks at the page*)

GEORGE (*Laments*): Connect, George.
> (*Trails off*)

Connect . . .
> (FRIEDA *and* JULES *enter. They seem to be hiding*)

FRIEDA: Are you certain you wish to do this?

JULES (*Uncertain*): Of course. We just have to find a quiet spot. I've wanted to do it outside for a long time.

FRIEDA: Franz would kill you —

JULES (*Panics*): Is he in the park?

FRIEDA: I am not certain.

JULES: Oh. Well. Perhaps some other day would be better.

FRIEDA: Some other day? Always some other day. Perhaps you do not really wish to —

JULES (*Subservient*): I do. I do! I love tall grass.

FRIEDA: *Ja.* Tall grass. You wouldn't toy with my affections, would you?

JULES: No. No. Of course not.

82

FRIEDA: I see a quiet spot over there.

JULES (*Pointing where she did, nervous*): Over there. There are people in that grove —
    (FRIEDA *places his hand on her breast. They are interrupted by the entrance of* CELESTE #2 *and the* SOLDIER. FRIEDA, *then* JULES, *exits; as he leaves*)
Bon jour.

SOLDIER: Do you suppose there is a violation being perpetrated by that man?

CELESTE #2: What?

SOLDIER: There is something in the air today . . .

CELESTE #1 (*To the* COMPANION): Being alone is nothing new for me.

SOLDIER (*Noticing* CELESTE #1): Look who is watching us.

CELESTE #1: Sundays are such a bore. I'd almost rather be in the shop. Do you like your work? I hate mine!

CELESTE #2: I do not care if she never speaks to me again.

SOLDIER: She won't.
    (*Chord.* FRANZ *and the* NURSE *enter as if to rendezvous*)

YVONNE (*Entering*): FRANZ!
        (NURSE *exits.* YVONNE *goes to* FRANZ)
Franz, have you seen Louise?

FRANZ (*Angry*): *Nein*, Madame.

YVONNE: I thought Frieda was going to care for her today.

FRANZ: But it's Sunday.

YVONNE: What of it?

FRANZ: Our day off!

YVONNE: Oh. But I have just lost my little girl!

83

(FRANZ *shrugs his shoulders and begins looking for* LOUISE)

SOLDIER: Let's go say hello to Celeste.

YVONNE (*Calling*): Louise?

CELESTE #2 (*Indignant*): I do not wish to speak with her!

SOLDIER: Come. It will be fun!
> (SOLDIER *takes* CELESTE #2 *toward* CELESTE #1. LOUISE *comes running in, breathless. She immediately goes to* YVONNE *'s side*)

YVONNE: Louise! Where have you been, young lady?!

LOUISE: With Frieda.

YVONNE (*To* FRANZ): There, you see.

FRANZ: Frieda?

LOUISE: And with Father.

YVONNE: Your father is in the studio.

LOUISE: No, he's not. He's with Frieda. I saw them.

FRANZ: Where?

LOUISE: Over there. Tonguing.
> (FRANZ *exits. Music under, agitated*)

OLD LADY: Manners. Grace. Respect.

YVONNE (*Beginning to spank* LOUISE): How dare you, young lady!

LOUISE:	(SOLDIER *and* CELESTE #2
It's true. It's true!	*reach* CELESTE #1)
	CELESTE #1:
	What do you want?
(JULES *enters, somewhat*	
sheepishly)	SOLDIER:
	We've come for a visit.

84

YVONNE:
Where the hell have you been? What are you doing here?

JULES:
Darling, I came out here looking for Louise.

LOUISE:
(*Crying*)
You came to tongue.

CELESTE #1:
I don't want to say hello to her. Cheap Christmas wrapping.

CELESTE #2:
Cheap! Look who is talking. You have the worst reputation of anyone in Paris.

CELESTE #1:
At least I have a reputation. You could not draw a fly to flypaper!

(BOATMAN *enters and begins chasing* LOUISE *around the stage.* MR. *and* MRS. *enter and are caught up in the frenzy. All hell breaks loose, everyone speaking at once, the stage erupting into total chaos*)

YVONNE:
How dare you, Jules!
(*She goes to him and begins striking him*)

JULES:
Nothing, I swear.

YVONNE:
Nothing. Look.
(FRANZ *drags in* FRIEDA)

Have you been with my husband?

SOLDIER:
Ladies, you mustn't fight.

CELESTE #2:
I seem to be doing just fine.

CELESTE #1:
Hah. With a diseased soldier!

SOLDIER:
Wait just a minute.

FRIEDA:
Madame, he gave me no
choice.

FRANZ:
What do you mean he gave
you no choice?

JULES:
(*Letting go of* LOUISE, *who
drifts off to the side*)
That is not so. Your wife
lured me.

FRIEDA:
Lured you! You all but
forced me —

JULES:
You are both fired!

FRANZ:
FIRED! You think we would
continue to work in your
house?

YVONNE:
Jules, you cannot change the
subject. What were you
doing?

CELESTE #1:
Disgusting sores every-
where.

CELESTE #2:
Don't say that about him.

SOLDIER:
Yes, don't say that —

CELESTE #1:
I'll say whatever I like.
You are both ungrateful,
cheap, ugly, diseased,
disgusting garbage . . .

SOLDIER:
Listen here, lady, if in
fact there is anything
ladylike about you. You
should be glad to take what
you can get, any way you
can get it and I —

CELESTE #2:
You think you know every-
thing. You are not so
special, and far from as
pretty as you think, and
everyone that comes into
the shop knows exactly what
you are and what —

(*Everyone has slowly fought their way to the middle of the
stage, creating one big fight.* GEORGE *and the* OLD LADY

86

have been watching the chaos. GEORGE *begins to cross stage to exit. Arpeggiated chord, as at the beginning of the play. Everybody suddenly freezes in place)*

OLD LADY: Remember, George.
>   *(Another chord.* GEORGE *turns to the group)*

GEORGE: Order.
>   *(Another chord. Everyone turns simultaneously to* GEORGE. *As chords continue under, he nods to them, and they each take up a position on stage)*

Design.
>   *(Chord.* GEORGE *nods to* FRIEDA *and* FRANZ, *and they cross downstage right onto the apron. Chord.* GEORGE *nods to* MR. *and* MRS., *and they cross upstage)*

Tension.
>   *(Chord.* GEORGE *nods to* CELESTE #1 *and* CELESTE #2, *and they cross downstage. Another chord.* JULES *and* YVONNE *cross upstage)*

Balance.
>   *(Chord.* OLD LADY *crosses right as* DOT *and* LOUIS *cross center.* GEORGE *signals* LOUIS *away from* DOT. *Another chord.* SOLDIER *crosses upstage left;* LOUISE, *upstage right. Chord.* GEORGE *gestures to the* BOATMAN, *who crosses downstage right)*

Harmony.
>   *(The music becomes calm, stately, triumphant.* GEORGE *turns front. The promenade begins. Throughout the song,* GEORGE *is moving about, setting trees, cut-outs, and fig-ures — making a perfect picture)*

ALL *(Sing):*
Sunday,
By the blue
Purple yellow red water
On the green
Purple yellow red grass,

Let us pass
Through our perfect park,
Pausing on a Sunday
By the cool
Blue triangular water
On the soft
Green elliptical grass
As we pass
Through arrangements of shadows
Towards the verticals of trees
Forever . . .
                    (*The horn sounds*)
By the blue
Purple yellow red water
On the green
Orange violet mass
Of the grass
In our perfect park,

GEORGE (*To* DOT):
Made of flecks of light
And dark,
And parasols:
Bumbum bum bumbumbum
Bumbum bum . . .

ALL:
People strolling through the trees
Of a small suburban park
On an island in the river
On an ordinary Sunday . . .
      (*The horn sounds. Chimes. They all reach their positions*)
Sunday . . .
      (*The horn again. Everyone assumes the final pose of the
      painting.* GEORGE *comes out to the apron*)
Sunday . . .

(At the last moment, GEORGE *rushes back and removes* LOUISE*'s eyeglasses. He dashes back on to the apron and freezes the picture. Final chord. The completed canvas flies in. Very slow fade, as the image of the characters fades behind the painting with* GEORGE *in front. Blackout)*

GEORGE: "White. A blank page or canvas. The challenge: bring order to the whole."

George (Mandy Patinkin)

MARTHA SWOPE

George (Mandy Patinkin) and Dot (Bernadette Peters)

"Sunday in the Park with George"
Dot (Bernadette Peters)

Dot (Bernadette Peters), George (Mandy Patinkin),
Nurse (Judith Moore) and Old Lady (Barbara Bryne)

MARTHA SWOPE

95

Yvonne (Dana Ivey), Jules (Charles Kimbrough) and the *tableau vivant* of Seurat's painting "Une Baignade Asnières" ("Bathing at Asnières")

97

DOT: "I'd be in the Follies"
Dot (Bernadette Peters)

Seurat's "Jeune Femme se Poudrant"
("Woman Powdering Herself")

"Color and Light"
George (Mandy Patinkin) and Dot (Bernadette Peters)

Mr. and Mrs. (Kurt Knudson and Judith Moore)

"Everybody Loves Louis"
Louis (Cris Groenendaal) and Dot (Bernadette Peters)

MARTHA SWOPE

103

Freida (Nancy Opel) and Franz (Brent Spiner); in background, Celeste #1 (Melanie Vaughan), Celeste #2 (Mary D'Arcy), Nurse (Judith Moore) Companion, Soldier (Robert Westenberg) and Jules (Charles Kimbrough)

MARTHA SWOPE

George (Mandy Patinkin) sketching the Boatman (William Parry); in background, Yvonne (Dana Ivey), Louise (Danielle Ferland), Jules (Charles Kimbrough), Nurse (Judith Moore), Old Lady (Barbara Bryne), Louis (Cris Groenendaal) and Dot (Bernadette Peters)

"Finishing the Hat"
George (Mandy Patinkin)

107

"Beautiful"
Old Lady (Barbara Brync) and George (Mandy Patinkin)

Companion, Celeste #1 (Melanie Vaughan), Soldier
(Robert Westenberg), Celeste #2 (Mary D'Arcy)

George (Mandy Patinkin) freezes the tableau

MARTHA SWOPE

111

George (Mandy Patinkin) in front of the finished painting

113

Georges Seurat (1859-1891)

The presentation of Chromolume #7 with Marie (Bernadette Peters, *far left*) and George (Mandy Patinkin, *far right*)

"Putting It Together"
George (Mandy Patinkin), Elaine (Mary D'Arcy) and Marie
(Bernadette Peters), with a cut-out of George at far left

116

MARTHA SWOPE

117

"Children and Art"
George (Mandy Patinkin) and Marie (Bernadette Peters)

"Move On"
George (Mandy Patinkin) and Dot (Bernadette Peters)

Marie Friedman as Dot and Philip Quast
as George in the London production

ACT II

Lights fade up slowly, and we see everyone in the tableau. There is a very long pause before we begin. The audience should feel the tension. Finally, music begins. One by one, they sing.

DOT:
It's hot up here.

YVONNE:
It's hot and it's monotonous.

LOUISE:
I want my glasses.

FRANZ:
This is not my good profile.

NURSE: Nobody can even *see* my profile.

CELESTE #1:
I hate this dress.

CELESTE #2:
The soldiers have forgotten us.

FRIEDA:
The boatman *schwitzes.*

JULES: I am completely out of proportion.

SOLDIER:

   These helmets weigh a lot on us.

OLD LADY:

   This tree is blocking my view.

LOUISE:

   I can't see anything.

BOATMAN:

   Why are they complaining?
   It could have been raining.

DOT:

   I hate these people.

ALL:

   It's hot up here
   A lot up here.
   It's hot up here
   Forever.

   A lot of fun
   It's not up here.
   It's hot up here,
   No matter what.

   There's not a breath
   Of air up here,
   And they're up here
   Forever.

   It's not my fault
   I got up here.
   I'll rot up here,
   I am so hot up here.

YVONNE (*To* LOUISE): Darling, don't clutch mother's hand
   quite so tightly. Thank you.

124

CELESTE #1:

It's hot up here.

FRIEDA:

At least you have a parasol.

SOLDIER, NURSE, YVONNE, *and* LOUISE:

Well, look who's talking,

Sitting in the shade.

JULES (*To* DOT): I trust my cigar is not bothering you —
unfortunately, it never goes out.

(*She pays him no attention*)

You have excellent concentration.

SOLDIER (*To* COMPANION):

It's good to be together again.

CELESTE #2 (*To* CELESTE #1):

See, I told you they were odd.

CELESTE #1:

Don't slouch.

LOUISE:

He took my glasses!

YVONNE:

You've been eating something sticky.

NURSE:

I put on rouge today, too . . .

FRIEDA (*To* BOATMAN):

Don't you ever take a bath?

OLD LADY:

Nurse! Hand me my fan.

NURSE:

I can't.

FRANZ:
  At least the brat is with her mother.

LOUISE:
  I heard that!

JULES (*To* DOT):
  Do you like tall grass?

FRIEDA:
  Hah!

YVONNE:
  Jules!

BOATMAN:
  Bunch of animals . . .

DOT:
  I hate these people.

ALL:
  It's hot up here
  And strange up here,
  No change up here
  Forever.

  How still it is,
  How odd it is,
  And God, it is
  So hot!

SOLDIER: I like the one in the light hat.

DOT: /
  Hello, George.
  I do not wish to be remembered
  Like this, George,
  With them, George.
  My hem, George:

126

Three inches off the ground
And then this monkey
And these people, George —

They'll argue till they fade
And whisper things and grunt.
But thank you for the shade,
And putting me in front.
Yes, thank you, George, for that . . .
And for the hat . . .

CELESTE #1:
 It's hot up here.

YVONNE:
 It's hot and it's monotonous.

LOUISE:
 I want my glasses!

FRANZ:
 This is not my good profile.

CELESTE #1:
 I hate this dress.

(Overlapping)

CELESTE #2:
 The soldiers have forgotten us.

CELESTE #1:
 Don't slouch!

BOATMAN:
 Animals . . .

JULES:
 Are you sure you don't like tall grass?

NURSE:
 I put on rouge today, too . . .

127

FRIEDA:
Don't you ever take a bath?

SOLDIER:
It's good to be together again.

OLD LADY:
Nurse, hand me my fan.

DOT:
It's hot up here.

YVONNE:
It's hot and it's monotonous.

LOUISE:
He took my glasses, I want my glasses!

FRANZ:
This is not my good profile.

ALL:
And furthermore,
Finding you're
Fading
Is very degrading
And God, I am so hot!

Well, there are worse things than sweating
By a river on a Sunday.
There are worse things than sweating by a river

BOATMAN:
When you're sweating in a picture
That was painted by a genius

FRANZ:
And you know that you're immortal

FRIEDA:
And you'll always be remembered

NURSE:
  Even if they never see you

OLD LADY:
  And you're listening to drivel

SOLDIER:
  And you're part of your companion

LOUISE:
  And your glasses have been stolen

YVONNE:
  And you're bored beyond endurance

LOUIS:
  And the baby has no diapers

CELESTE #1 (*To* CELESTE #2):
  And you're slouching

CELESTE #2:
  I am not!

JULES:
  And you are out of all proportion!

DOT:
  And I hate these people!

ALL:
  You never get
  A breeze up here,
  And she's (he's) up here
  Forever.

  You cannot run
  Amok up here,
  You're stuck up here
  In this gavotte.

  Perspectives don't

129

Make sense up here.
It's tense up here
Forever.

The outward show
Of bliss up here
Is disappear-
Ing dot by dot.
    (*Long pause. Music continues for a long moment*)
And it's hot!
    (*They shake themselves loose from the pose for a brief
    moment, but at the last beat of the music resume their posi-
    tions.* GEORGE *enters downstage and stands on the apron
    in front of the tableau*)

GEORGE: A fascination with light. The bedroom where I
slept as a child — it had a window. At night, the reflec-
tion of the light — that is, the light outside the window
— created a shadow-show on my wall. So it was, lying in
my bed, looking at the wall, I was able to make out shapes
of night activity from the street. These images were not
rich in detail, so my mind's eye filled in the shapes to
bring them to life. Straying from the point. The point?
Light and sleep. I didn't sleep. Well, of course I slept, but
always when there was a choice, when I might fight the
urge, I would lie awake, eyes fixed on the wall, sometimes
until the bright sunlight of the morning washed the
image away. Off and running. Off and running. First
into the morning light. Last on the gas-lit streets. Energy
that had no time for sleep. A mission to see, to record
impressions. Seeing . . . recording . . . seeing the record,
then feeling the experience. Connect the dots, George.
Slowing to a screeching halt — in one week. Fighting to
wake up. "Wake up, Georgie." I can still feel her cool
hand on my warm cheek. Could darkness be an inviting
place? Could sleep surpass off and running? No. Lying

still, I can see the boys swimming in the Seine. I can see them all, on a sunny Sunday in the park.

(*He exits. During the following, the characters break from their poses when they speak. Accompanying their exits, pieces of scenery disappear; by the time the* BOATMAN *exits at the end of the sequence, the set is returned to its original white configuration*)

CELESTE #2: Thirty-one . . .

CELESTE #1: It is hard to believe.

CELESTE #2: Yes.

CELESTE #1: It seems like only yesterday we were posing for him.

CELESTE #2: We never posed for him!

CELESTE #1: Certainly we did! We are in a painting, aren't we?

CELESTE #2: It's not as if he asked us to sit!

CELESTE #1: If you had sat up —

SOLDIER: Will you two just keep QUIET!
(*He steps downstage. The* CELESTES *exit*)
I hardly knew the man. I would spend my Sundays here, and I would see him sketching, so I was surprised when he stopped showing up. Of course, I did not notice right away. But one day, I realized, something was different — like a flash of light, right through me, the way that man would stare at you when he sketched — I knew, he was no longer.

(SOLDIER *exits.* LOUISE *breaks away from her mother and dashes downstage*)

LOUISE: I am going to be a painter when I grow up!

BOATMAN: If you live.
(LOUISE *runs off*)

131

FRIEDA: Honestly!

BOATMAN: Keep your mouth shut!

FRIEDA: It is my mouth and I shall do as I please!

FRANZ: Quiet! George was a gentleman.

FRIEDA: Soft spoken.

FRANZ: And he was a far superior artist to Monsieur.

FRIEDA: George had beautiful eyes.

FRANZ: *Ja,* he — beautiful eyes?

FRIEDA: *Ja* . . . well . . . eyes that captured beauty.

FRANZ (*Suspicious*): *Ja* . . . he chose his subjects well.
(*They exit*)

DOT: I was in Charleston when I heard. At first, I was surprised by the news. Almost relieved, in fact. Perhaps I knew this is how it would end — perhaps we both knew.
(*She exits*)

OLD LADY: A parent wants to die first. But George was always off and running, and I was never able to keep up with him.

NURSE: No one knew he was ill until the very last days. I offered to care for him, but he would let no one near. Not even her.
(OLD LADY *and* NURSE *exit*)

JULES (*Too sincere*): George had great promise as a painter. It really is a shame his career was ended so abruptly. He had an unusual flair for color and light, and his work was not as mechanical as some have suggested. I liked George. He was dedicated to his work — seldom did anything but work — and I am proud to have counted him among my friends.

132

YVONNE: George stopped me once in the park — it was the only time I had ever spoken to him outside the company of Jules. He stared at my jacket for an instant, then muttered something about beautiful colors and just walked on. I rather fancied George.

(JULES *looks at her*)

Well, most of the women did!

(JULES *and* YVONNE *exit*)

BOATMAN: They all wanted him and hated him at the same time. They wanted to be painted — splashed on some fancy salon wall. But they hated him, too. Hated him because he only spoke when he absolutely had to. Most of all, they hated him because they knew he would always be around.

(BOATMAN *exits. The stage is bare.*)

(*Lights change. Electronic music. It is 1984. We are in the auditorium of the museum where the painting now hangs. Enter* GEORGE. *He wheels in his grandmother,* MARIE *[played by* DOT*], who is ninety-eight and confined to a wheelchair.* DENNIS, GEORGE's *technical assistant, rolls on a control console and places it stage right. An immense white machine rolls on and comes to rest center stage. Our contemporary* GEORGE *is an inventor-sculptor, and this is his latest invention,* Chromolume #7. *The machine is postmodern in design and is dominated by a four-foot-in-diameter sphere at the top. It glows a range of cool colored light.* MARIE *sits on one side of the machine, and* GEORGE *stands at the console on the other. Behind them is a full-stage projection screen*)

GEORGE: Ladies and gentlemen, in 1983 I was commissioned by this museum to create an art piece commemorating Georges Seurat's painting "A Sunday Afternoon on the Island of La Grande Jatte." My latest Chromolume

133

stands before you now, the seventh in a continuing series. Because I have a special association with this painting, the museum director, Robert Greenberg, suggested I assemble a short presentation to precede the activation of my latest invention. I have brought my grandmother along to give me a hand.

(Introducing her)

My grandmother, Marie.

(What follows is a coordinated performance of music, text [read from index cards by GEORGE *and* MARIE*], film projections of the images referred to, and light emissions from the machine. The first section is accompanied by film projections)*

MARIE: I was born in Paris, France, ninety-eight years ago. My grandson, George.

GEORGE: I was born in Lodi, New Jersey, thirty-two years ago.

MARIE: My mother was married to Louis, a baker. They left France when I was an infant to travel to Charleston, South Carolina.

GEORGE: Georges Seurat.

MARIE: Born: December 2, 1859.

GEORGE: It was through his mother that the future artist was introduced to the lower-class Parisian parks. Seurat received a classical training at the Beaux Arts.

MARIE: Like his father, he was not an easy man to know.

GEORGE: He lived in an age when science was gaining influence over Romantic principles.

MARIE: He worked very hard.

GEORGE: His first painting, at the age of twenty-four, "Bathing at Asnières," was rejected by the Salon, but was shown by the Group of Independent Artists.

134

MARIE: They hung it over the refreshment stand.
(*Ad-libbing*)
Wasn't that awful?

GEORGE: On Ascension Day 1884, he began work on his second painting, "A Sunday Afternoon on the Island of La Grande Jatte." He was to work two years on this painting.

MARIE: He always knew where he was going before he picked up a paint brush.

GEORGE: He denied conventional perspective and conventional space.

MARIE: He was unconventional in his lifestyle as well.
(*Ad-libbing again*)
So was I! You know I was a Florodora Girl for a short time — when I left Charleston and before I was married to my first husband —

GEORGE (*Interrupting her*): Marie. Marie!
(*She looks over to him*)
The film is running.

MARIE: Excuse me.
(*She reads*)
They hung it over the refreshment stand.

GEORGE: Marie!
(*He reads*)
Having studied scientific findings on color, he developed a new style of painting. He found by painting tiny particles, color next to color, that at a certain distance the eye would fuse the specks optically, giving them greater intensity than any mixed pigments.

MARIE: He wanted to paint with colored lights.

GEORGE: Beams of colored light, he hoped.

135

MARIE: It was shown at the Eighth and last Impressionist Exhibition.

GEORGE: Monet, Renoir, and Sisley withdrew their submissions because of his painting.

MARIE: They placed it in a small room off to the side of the main hall, too dark for the painting to truly be seen.

GEORGE: The painting was ridiculed by most. But there were also a handful of believers in his work.

MARIE: He went on to paint six more major paintings before his sudden death at the age of thirty-one. He never sold a painting in his lifetime.

GEORGE: On this occasion, I present my latest Chromolume —

MARIE: — Number Seven —

GEORGE: — which pays homage to "La Grande Jatte" and to my grandmother, Marie. The score for this presentation has been composed by Naomi Eisen.
(NAOMI *enters, bows, and exits*)

MARIE (*She reads a stage direction by mistake*): George begins to activate the Chromolume machine as . . .

GEORGE: Don't read that part, Grandmother.

MARIE: Oh . . . don't read this . . .
(*Music begins to increase in volume and intensity. Strobe lights begin emitting from the machine along with side shafts of brilliant light. Colors begin to fill the stage and audience, creating a pointillist look. Just as the sphere begins to illuminate, producing various images from the painting, there is a sudden explosion of sparks and smoke. The lighting system flickers on and off until everything dies, including music. There is a moment of silence in the darkness*)

136

GEORGE (*Under his breath*): Shit.
(*Calling out*)
Robert Greenberg?

GREENBERG (*From the back of the house*): Just a minute, George!
(*Some light returns to the smoke-filled stage*)

DENNIS (*Offstage*): It's the regulator, George.
(*Lights come up on* GEORGE, *who is looking inside the machine. He steps downstage toward the audience*)

GEORGE: My apologies, ladies and gentlemen. For precise synchronization of all the visual elements, I've installed a new state-of-the-art Japanese microcomputer which controls the voltage regulator. I think that the surge from the musical equipment has created an electrical short.
(*Beat*)
Unfortunately, no electricity, no art. Give us a moment and we'll be able to bypass the regulator and be back in business.
(*After "no electricity, no art," GREENBERG has entered and stands to the side of the apron. DENNIS enters and joins* GEORGE *at the Chromolume*)

GREENBERG: I am very sorry, ladies and gentlemen. We seem to be having a little electrical difficulty.
(NAOMI *has entered and rushed to the machine*)

NAOMI: There's no juice!

GREENBERG: You must realize this is the first time we have had a collaboration like this at the museum and it has offered some extraordinary challenges to us here.
(NAOMI *and* DENNIS *exit arguing*)
Now, I hope to see all of you at the reception and dinner which will follow the presentation. It's right down the hall in the main gallery, where the painting hangs. And we have a very special treat for you. As I am sure you have

137

noticed, in order to raise additional funds we have chosen to sell the air rights to the museum — and some of the twenty-seven flights of condominiums that stand above us now will be open for your inspection after dinner. You may even wish to become one of our permanent neighbors!

GEORGE: We're ready, Bob.

GREENBERG: Well . . . proceed. Proceed!
(*He exits*)

GEORGE (*Into his headset*): Dennis! Lights.
(*Lights dim and the presentation continues. Music gathers momentum. The Chromolume begins several seconds before the speaking resumes, with images from the painting projected on its sphere, illustrating the lecture*)

MARIE: When I was young, Mother loved telling me tales of her life in France, and of her work as an artist's model.

GEORGE: Her mother showed her this great painting and pointed to this woman and said that it was she.

MARIE: And she pointed to a couple in the back — they were holding an infant child — and she said that was me!

GEORGE: Shortly before my great-grandmother's death, she spoke of her association with the artist of this painting. She told Marie that Seurat was her real father.

MARIE: I was shocked!

GEORGE: My parents never believed this story. After all, there was no proof. I do not —

MARIE (*Produces a red book, unbeknownst to* GEORGE): My mother gave me this small red book.

GEORGE: Marie!

MARIE: Oh, George, I wanted to bring the book and show it.

(To audience)
In the back are notes about his great-grandfather, the artist.

GEORGE: Actually, this book is really just a grammar book in the handwriting of a child, and though there *are* notes in the back which mention a Georges — they could be referring to anyone.

MARIE: But they do not.

GEORGE: I do not know that there is any validity to this story.

MARIE: Of course there is validity!
(To the audience)
He has to have everything spelled out for him!

GEORGE: The facts are sketchy. The tales are many. I would like to invite you into *my* "Sunday: Island of Light." It will be on exhibition here in the upstairs gallery for three weeks.
(Music crescendos, as laser beams burst over the audience. When they complete their course, the sphere begins to turn, sending out a blinding burst of light. The painting flies in)

(We are now in the gallery where the painting hangs and in front of which the reception is beginning. HARRIET *and* BILLY *enter, closely followed by* REDMOND, GREENBERG, ALEX, BETTY, *and* NAOMI. *Cocktail music under)*

BILLY: Well, I can't say that *I* understand what that light machine has to do with this painting.

HARRIET: Darling, it's a theme and variation.

BILLY: Oh. Theme and variation.

GREENBERG *(To* REDMOND*)*: Times change so quickly.

REDMOND: Lord knows.

GREENBERG: That's the challenge of our work. You never

know what movement is going to hit next. Which artist to embrace.

(*Rhumba music*)

NAOMI: I thought it went very well, except for that electrical screw-up. What did you guys think?

ALEX:	BETTY:
Terrible.	Terrific.

(*Short embarrassed pause*)

HARRIET (*Sings*):
I mean, I don't understand completely —

BILLY (*Sings*):
I'm not surprised.

HARRIET:
But he combines all these different trends.

BILLY:
I'm not surprised.

HARRIET:
You can't divide art today
Into categories neatly —

BILLY:
Oh.

HARRIET:
What matters is the means, not the ends.

BILLY:
I'm not surprised.

HARRIET *and* BILLY:
That is the state of the art, my dear,
That is the state of the art.

GREENBERG (*Sings*):
It's not enough knowing good from rotten —

REDMOND (*Sings*):
   You're telling me —

GREENBERG:
   When something new pops up every day.

REDMOND:
   You're telling me —

GREENBERG:
   It's only new, though, for now —

REDMOND:
   Nouveau.

GREENBERG:
   But yesterday's forgotten.

REDMOND (*Nods*):
   And tomorrow is already passé.

GREENBERG:
   There's no surprise.

REDMOND *and* GREENBERG:
   That is the state of the art, my friend,
   That is the state of the art.

BETTY (*Sings*):
   He's an original.

ALEX: Was.

NAOMI:
   I like the images.

ALEX: Some.

BETTY:
   Come on.
   You had your moment,
   Now it's George's turn —

ALEX (*Sings*):
    It's George's turn?
    I wasn't talking turns,
    I'm talking art.

BETTY (*To* NAOMI):
    Don't you think he's original?

NAOMI:
    Well, yes . . .

BETTY (*To* ALEX):
    You're talking crap.

ALEX (*Overlapping with* NAOMI):
    But is it really new?

NAOMI:
    Well, no . . .

ALEX (*To* BETTY):
    His own collaborator — !

BETTY (*Overlapping with* NAOMI):
    It's more than novelty.

NAOMI:
    Well, yes . . .

BETTY (*To* ALEX):
    It's just impersonal, but —

ALEX:
    It's all promotion, but then —

ALEX *and* BETTY (*To* NAOMI):
    That is the state of the art,
    Isn't it?

NAOMI (*Caught between them*):
    Well . . .

142

BILLY (*To* HARRIET):
   Art isn't easy —

HARRIET (*Nodding*):
   Even when you've amassed it —

BETTY:
   Fighting for prizes —

GREENBERG:
   No one can be an oracle.

REDMOND (*Nodding*):
   Art isn't easy.

ALEX:
   Suddenly —

                              (*Snaps fingers*)

   You're past it.

NAOMI:
   All compromises —

HARRIET (*To* BILLY):
   And then when it's allegorical — !

REDMOND *and* GREENBERG:
   Art isn't easy —

ALL:
   Any way you look at it.
      (*Chord, fanfare.* GEORGE *makes a grand entrance with*
      MARIE *and* ELAINE. *Applause from guests.* GEORGE *and*
      MARIE *move towards the painting. Lights come down on*
      GEORGE, *who sings*)

GEORGE:
   All right, George.
   As long as it's your night, George . . .
   You know what's in the room, George:

Another Chromolume, George.
It's time to get to work . . .
> (*Music continues under*)

MARIE: George, look. All these lovely people in front of our painting.

GREENBERG (*Coming up to* GEORGE): George, I want you to meet one of our board members.
> (*He steers* GEORGE *over to* BILLY *and* HARRIET)
This is Harriet Pawling.

HARRIET: What a pleasure. And this is my friend, Billy Webster.

BILLY: How do you do.

GREENBERG: Well, I'll just leave you three to chat.
> (*He exits*)

BILLY: Harriet was so impressed by your presentation.

HARRIET: This is the third piece of yours I've seen. They are getting so large!

BILLY: What heading does your work fall under?

GEORGE: Most people think of it as sculpture.

BILLY: Sculpture . . .

GEORGE: Actually, I think of myself as an inventor as well as a sculptor.

BILLY: It's so unconventional for sculpture.
> (*Lights down on* GEORGE)

GEORGE (*To audience and himself, sings*):
Say "cheese," George,
And put them at their ease, George.
You're up on the trapeze, George.
Machines don't grow on trees, George.

144

Start putting it together . . .
> (*Lights up*)

HARRIET: I bet your great-grandfather would be very proud!
> (*They are joined by* MARIE *and* ELAINE, *who have been nearby and overheard the conversation*)

MARIE: Yes. He would have loved this evening.

BILLY: How do you know?

MARIE: I just know. I'm like that.

HARRIET: Hi. I'm Harriet Pawling.

BILLY: Billy Webster.

MARIE: How do you do. This is Elaine — George's former wife.

ELAINE (*Embarrassed*): Hello.

MARIE: Elaine is such a darling, I will always think of her as my grand-daughter. I am so happy that these children have remained close. Isn't that nice?

BILLY: Yes. Harriet has just gone through a rather messy divorce —

HARRIET: Bill!
> (*Awkward pause*)

What a fascinating family you have!

MARIE: Many people say that. George and I are going back to France next month to visit the island where the painting was made, and George is going to bring the Lomochrome.
> (*Music*)

GEORGE: Chromolume. I've been invited by the government to do a presentation of the machine on the island.

MARIE: George has never been to France.

145

GEORGE (*Front, sings*):
Art isn't easy —
(*He raises a cut-out of himself in front of* BILLY *and* HARRI-
ET *and comes downstage*)
Even when you're hot.

BILLY (*To cut-out*): Are these inventions of yours one of a
kind?

GEORGE:
Advancing art is easy —
(*To* BILLY, *but front*)
Yes.
Financing it is not.

MARIE: They take a year to make.

GEORGE (*Front*):
A vision's just a vision
If it's only in your head.

MARIE: The minute he finishes one, he starts raising money
for the next.

GEORGE:
If no one gets to see it,
It's as good as dead.

MARIE: Work. Work. Work.

GEORGE:
It has to come to light!
(*Music continues under.* GEORGE *speaks as if to* BILLY *and*
HARRIET, *but away from them, and front*)
I put the names of my contributors on the side of each
machine.

ELAINE: Some very impressive people!

HARRIET: Well, we must speak further. My family has a foundation and we are always looking for new projects.

146

GEORGE (*Front, sings*):
  Bit by bit,
  Putting it together . . .

MARIE: Family — it's all you really have.

GEORGE:
  Piece by piece —
  Only way to make a work of art.
  Every moment makes a contribution,
  Every little detail plays a part.
  Having just the vision's no solution,
  Everything depends on execution:
  Putting it together —
  That's what counts.

HARRIET (*To cut-out*): Actually, the Board of the Foundation
  is meeting next week . . .

GEORGE:
  Ounce by ounce
  Putting it together . . .

HARRIET: You'll come to lunch.

GEORGE:
  Small amounts,
  Adding up to make a work of art.
  First of all, you need a good foundation,
  Otherwise it's risky from the start.
  Takes a little cocktail conversation,
  But without the proper preparation,
  Having just the vision's no solution,
  Everything depends on execution.

  The art of making art
  Is putting it together
  Bit by bit . . .
    (*The cut-out remains, as* BILLY *and* HARRIET *talk to it;*

147

GEORGE, *working away, is cornered by* CHARLES REDMOND.
Music continues under)

REDMOND: We have been hearing about you for some time. We haven't met. Charles Redmond. County Museum of Texas.

GEORGE: Nice to meet you.

REDMOND: Your work is just tremendous.

GEORGE: Thank you.

REDMOND: I don't mean to bring business up during a social occasion, but I wanted you to know we're in the process of giving out some very sizable commissions —

GREENBERG: You're not going to steal him away, are you?
  (GEORGE *signals and another cut-out of himself slides in from the wings. He leaves his drink in its hand, then steps forward*)

GEORGE:
  Link by link,
  Making the connections . . .
  Drink by drink,
  Fixing and perfecting the design.
  Adding just a dab of politician
  (Always knowing where to draw the line),
  Lining up the funds but in addition
  Lining up a prominent commission,
  Otherwise your perfect composition
  Isn't going to get much exhibition.

  Art isn't easy.
  Every minor detail
  Is a major decision.
  Have to keep things in scale,
  Have to hold to your vision —
              (*Pauses for a split second*)

148

Every time I start to feel defensive,
I remember lasers are expensive.
What's a little cocktail conversation
If it's going to get you your foundation,
Leading to a prominent commission
And an exhibition in addition?
  (*The guests promenade briefly, working the room, then sing*)

ALL (*Except* MARIE):
Art isn't easy —

ALEX *and* BETTY:
Trying to make connections —

ALL:
Who understands it — ?

HARRIET *and* BILLY:
Difficult to evaluate —

ALL:
Art isn't easy —

GREENBERG *and* REDMOND:
Trying to form collections —

ALL:
Always in transit —

NAOMI (*To whoever will listen*):
And then when you have to collaborate — !

ALL:
Art isn't easy,
Any way you look at it . . .
  (*Chord. Cocktail piano. During the above,* BLAIR DANIELS, *an art critic, has entered.* GEORGE *is approached by* LEE RANDOLPH *with* MARIE)

MARIE: George, you have to meet Mr. Randolph!

RANDOLPH: Hello! Lee Randolph. I handle the public relations for the museum.

GEORGE: How do you do.

(NAOMI *joins them*)

NAOMI: There you are, George! Hi, Marie.

(*To* RANDOLPH)

Naomi Eisen.

RANDOLPH: Delighted. You kids made quite a stir tonight.

NAOMI: You see, George — that electrical foul-up didn't hurt our reception.

RANDOLPH: There's a lot of opportunity for some nice press here.

(GEORGE *gestures; a third cut-out of himself rises in front of* NAOMI *and* RANDOLPH. GEORGE *steps forward and sings*)

GEORGE:

Dot by dot,
Building up the image.

(*Flash.* PHOTOGRAPHER *starts taking pictures of the cut-out*)

Shot by shot,
Keeping at a distance doesn't pay.
Still, if you remember your objective,
Not give all your privacy away —

(*Flash. Beat; he glances at the first cut-out*)

A little bit of hype can be effective,
Long as you can keep it in perspective.
After all, without some recognition
No one's going to give you a commission,
Which will cause a crack in the foundation.
You'll have wasted all that conversation.

(*Music stops suddenly as* DENNIS *comes over, disheveled and apologetic.* DENNIS *is something of a nerd*)

DENNIS: I am really sorry, George.

150

(Cocktail music)
I spoke with Naomi in great detail about how much electricity her synthesizer was going to use — I computed the exact voltage —

GEORGE: Dennis! It's okay.

DENNIS: The laser was beautiful, George.

GEORGE: It was, wasn't it? Now go get yourself a drink, Dennis. Mingle.

DENNIS: George. I have one more thing I wanted to talk to you about. I was going to wait — no, I'll wait —

GEORGE: What?

DENNIS: I'm quitting.
(Music stops suddenly)

GEORGE: Quitting?

DENNIS: I'm going back to NASA. There is just too much pressure in this line of work.

GEORGE: Dennis, don't make any rash decisions. Relax, sleep on it, and we'll talk about it tomorrow.

DENNIS: Okay, George.

GEORGE (*Front, sings, music under*):
Art isn't easy . . .
(ALEX *and* BETTY *approach*)

BETTY: Hey, it's the brains.

GEORGE:
Even if you're smart . . .

ALEX: Little technical screw-up tonight, Dennis?
(DENNIS exits)

GEORGE:
You think it's all together,

151

And something falls apart . . .
> (*Music continues under*)

BETTY: I love the new machine, George.

GEORGE: Thanks. That means a lot to me.

ALEX: We saw you talking to Redmond from Texas.

GEORGE: Yeah.

BETTY: Did you get one of the commissions?

GEORGE: We talked about it. You guys?

ALEX: Her. My stuff is a little too inaccessible.

GEORGE: I love your work, Alex. I'll put in a good word for you.

ALEX (*Defensive*): He knows my work!

GEORGE (*Uncomfortable*): It's all politics, Alex. Maybe if you just lightened up once in a while.

BETTY (*Mollifying*): Texas would be fun!
> (GEORGE *beckons and a fourth cut-out slides in and heads toward* BETTY *and* ALEX)

GEORGE (*Front, sings*):
Art isn't easy.
> (*Gesturing towards* ALEX)

Overnight you're a trend,
You're the right combination —
> (*Behind him, cut-out #1 begins sinking slowly into the floor*)

Then the trend's at an end,
You're suddenly last year's sensation . . .
> (*Notices the cut-out, goes to raise it during the following*)

So you should support the competition,
Try to set aside your own ambition,
Even while you jockey for position —

(Cut-out #4 has slid in too far, and BETTY *and* ALEX *have turned away;* GEORGE, *unflustered, spins it back around towards* BETTY *and* ALEX, *who resume talking to it)*
If you feel a sense of coalition,
Then you never really stand alone.
If you want your work to reach fruition,
What you need's a link with your tradition,
And of course a prominent commission,
    (Cut-out #1 starts to sink again; GEORGE *hastens to fix it)*
Plus a little formal recognition,
So that you can go on exhibit —
                (Getting flustered)
So that your work can go on exhibition —
    (Loud promenade, very brief, during which cut-out #1 starts to go again, but stops just as GEORGE *reaches it. As he does so,* BLAIR DANIELS *comes up to him. Chords under)*

BLAIR: There's the man of the hour.

GEORGE: Blair. Hello. I just read your piece on Neo-Expressionism —

BLAIR: Just what the world needs — another piece on Neo-Expressionism.

GEORGE: Well, I enjoyed it.
    (Chords continue under, irregularly)

BLAIR: Good for you! Now, I had no idea you might be related to nineteenth-century France.

GEORGE: It's a cloudy ancestral line at best.

BLAIR: I'm dying to meet your grandmother. It was fun seeing the two of you onstage with your invention. It added a certain humanity to the proceedings.

GEORGE: Humanity?

BLAIR: George. Chromolume Number Seven?

GEORGE (*Sings to himself*):
Be nice, George . . .
>   (*Gestures for a cut-out; it doesn't rise*)

BLAIR: I was hoping it would be series of three — four at the most.

GEORGE:
You have to pay a price, George . . .
>   (*Gestures again; nothing*)

BLAIR: We have been there before, you know.

GEORGE: You never suffer from a shortage of opinions, do you, Blair?

BLAIR: You never minded my opinions when they were in your favor!

BLAIR:	GEORGE:
I have touted your work from the beginning, you know that. You were really on to something with these light machines — once. Now they're just becoming more and more about less and less.	They like to give Advice, George — (*Gestures offstage; nothing*) Don't think about it Twice, George . . . (*Gestures again; nothing*)

GEORGE: I disagree.
>   (*Music.* BLAIR *turns briefly away from him, rummaging through her purse for a cigarette.* GEORGE *takes advantage of this to rush offstage and bring on cut-out #5, which he sets up in front of her during the following*)

BLAIR: Don't get me wrong. You're a talented guy. If you weren't, I wouldn't waste our time with my opinions. I think you are capable of far more. Not that you couldn't succeed by doing Chromolume after Chromolume — but there are new discoveries to be made, George.

(She holds up her cigarette and waits for a light from the cut-out)

GEORGE *(Increasingly upset)*:
Be new, George.
They tell you till they're blue, George:
You're new or else you're through, George,
And even if it's true, George —
You do what you can do . . .

(Wandering among cut-outs, checking them)
Bit by bit,
Putting it together.
Piece by piece,
Working out the vision night and day.
All it takes is time and perseverance,
With a little luck along the way,
Putting in a personal appearance,
Gathering supporters and adherents . . .

(Music stops. BLAIR, getting impatient for her light, leaves the cut-out to join another group. GEORGE notices. Beat)

HARRIET *(To BILLY)*:
. . . But he combines all these different trends . . .

(Beat. The cut-out with HARRIET and BILLY falters)

GEORGE *(Moving to it smoothly as music resumes)*:
Mapping out the right configuration,
                    (Adjusting it)
Starting with a suitable foundation . . .

BETTY:
. . . He's an original . . .

ALEX:
. . . Was . . .

(During the following, all the cut-outs falter sporadically, causing GEORGE to move more and more rapidly among them)

155

GEORGE:

    Lining up a prominent commission —
    And an exhibition in addition —
    Here a little dab of politician —
    There a little touch of publication —
    Till you have a balanced composition —
    Everything depends on preparation —
    Even if you do have the suspicion
    That it's taking all your concentration —

(Simultaneously, with GEORGE)

BETTY:

    I like those images.

ALEX:

    Some.

BETTY:

    They're just his personal response.

ALEX:

    To what?

BETTY:

    The painting!

ALEX:

    Bullshit. Anyway, the painting's overrated . . .

BETTY:

    Overrated? It's a masterpiece!

ALEX:

    A masterpiece? Historically important, maybe —

BETTY:

    Oh, now you're judging Seurat, are you?

ALEX:

    All it is is pleasant, just like George's work.

156

BETTY:

It's just your jealousy of George's work.

ALEX:

No nuance, no resonance, no relevance —

BETTY:

There's nuance and there's resonance, there's relevance —

ALEX:

There's not much point in arguing.
Besides, it's all promotion, but then —

BETTY:

There's not much point in arguing.
You say it's all promotion, but then —

GREENBERG:

It's only new, though, for now,
And yesterday's forgotten.
Today it's all a matter of promotion,
But then —

REDMOND:

Nouveau.
And yesterday's forgotten
And you can't tell good from rotten
And today it's all a matter of promotion,
But then —

HARRIET:

You can't divide art today.
Go with it!
What will they think of next?

BILLY:

I'm not surprised.
What will they think of next?

OTHERS:

Most art today
Is a matter of promotion, but then —

157

GEORGE:

The art of making art	ALL:
Is putting it together —	That is the state of the art —
Bit by bit —	
Link by link —	
Drink by drink —	
Mink by mink —	And art isn't easy.
And that	
Is the state	
Of the	

ALL:

Art!

> (GEORGE *frames the successfully completed picture of the guests and cut-outs with his hands, as at the end of Act I. As soon as he exits, however, the cut-outs collapse and disappear.* MARIE *is over at the painting; She is joined by* HARRIET *and* BILLY)

GREENBERG: Ladies and gentlemen, dinner is served.
> (*Most of the party exits*)

HARRIET (*To* MARIE): Excuse me, could you please tell me: what is that square form up there?

BLAIR (*Who has been standing nearby*): That is a baby carriage.

MARIE: Who told you that?!

BLAIR: I'm sorry to butt in. I'm Blair Daniels and I've been waiting for the opportunity to tell you how much I enjoyed seeing you on stage.

MARIE: Why, thank you. But, my dear, that is not a baby carriage. That is Louis' waffle stove.

BLAIR: Waffle stove? I've read all there is to read about this work, and there's never been any mention of a waffle stove!

MARIE (*Indicating red book*): I have a book, too. My mother's.

158

It is a family legacy, as is this painting. And my mother often spoke of Louis' waffle stove!

BLAIR: Louis. Yes, you mentioned him in your presentation.
(GEORGE *re-enters; stays off to one side*)

MARIE: Family. You know, it is all you really have.

BILLY: You said that before.

MARIE: I say it often.

HARRIET: Excuse us.
(HARRIET *and* BILLY *exit*)

MARIE: You know, Miss Daniels, there are only two worthwhile things to leave behind when you depart this world: children and art. Isn't that correct?

BLAIR: I never quite thought of it that way.
(ELAINE *joins them*)

MARIE: Do you know Elaine?

BLAIR: No. I don't believe we've met. Blair Daniels.

ELAINE: I've heard a lot about you.

BLAIR: Oh, yes.

MARIE: Elaine and George were married once. I was so excited. I thought *they* might have a child. George and I are the only ones left, I'm afraid.
(*Whispers*)
I want George to have a child — continue the line. You can understand that, can't you, Elaine?

ELAINE: Of course.

MARIE: Are you married, Miss Daniels?

BLAIR: Awfully nice to have met you.
(*She shakes* MARIE*'s hand and exits*)

159

MARIE: Elaine, fix my chair so I can see Mama.
> (*She does.* ELAINE *crosses to* GEORGE)

ELAINE: George. I think Marie is a little too tired for the party. She seems to be slipping a bit.

GEORGE: I better take her back to the hotel.

ELAINE: I'll take her back. You stay.

GEORGE: Nah, it's a perfect excuse for me to leave early.

ELAINE: George. Don't be silly! You're the toast of the party. You should feel wonderful.

GEORGE (*Edgy*): Well, I don't feel wonderful.

ELAINE: Poor George. Well . . . tonight was a wonderful experience for Marie. I don't remember seeing her so happy. It was very good of you to include her.

GEORGE: She is something, isn't she?

ELAINE: Yes, she is . . .
> (ELAINE *begins to leave;* GEORGE *stops her; they embrace. Then she exits. The preceding has been underscored with the chords from Act I.* MARIE *has been staring up at the painting*)

MARIE (*Sings*):
You would have like him,
Mama, you would.
Mama, he makes things —
Mama, they're good.
Just as you said from the start:
Children and art . . .
> (*Starts nodding off*)
Children and art . . .
> (*Awakens with a start*)
He should be happy —

160

Mama, he's blue.
What do I do?

You should have seen it,
It was a sight!
Mama, I mean it —
All color and light — !
I don't understand what it was,
But, Mama, the things that he does:
They twinkle and shimmer and buzz —
You would have liked them . . .
                    (*Losing her train of thought*)
It . . .
Him . . .
                    (*Music continues, speaks*)
Henry . . . Henry? . . . Henry . . .

GEORGE (*Coming over*): It's George, Grandmother.

MARIE: Of course it is. I thought you were your father for a
moment.
                    (*Indicating painting*)
Did I tell you who that was?

GEORGE: Of course. That is your mother.

MARIE: That is correct.
                    (*Sings*)
Isn't she beautiful?
There she is —
                    (*Pointing to different figures*)
There she is, there she is, there she is —
Mama is everywhere,
He must have loved her so much . . .

GEORGE: Is she really in all those places, Marie?

MARIE:
This is our family —

This is the lot.
After I go, this is
All that you've got, honey —

GEORGE: Now, let's not have this discussion —

MARIE (*Before he can protest further*):
Wasn't she beautiful, though?

You would have liked her.
Mama did things
No one had done.
Mama was funny,
Mama was fun,
Mama spent money
When she had none.

Mama said, "Honey,
Mustn't be blue.
It's not so much do what you like
As it is that you like what you do."
Mama said, "Darling,
Don't make such a drama.
A little less thinking,
A little more feeling —"

GEORGE: Please don't start —

MARIE:
I'm just quoting Mama . . .
            (*Changing the subject, indicates* LOUISE)
The child is so sweet . . .
                    (*Indicates the* CELESTES *at center*)
And the girls are so rapturous . . .
Isn't it lovely how artists can capture us?

GEORGE: Yes, it is, Marie.

MARIE:
You would have liked her —

Honey, I'm wrong.
You would have loved her.

Mama enjoyed things.
Mama was smart.
See how she shimmers —
I mean from the heart.
             (ELAINE *enters and stands off to the side*)
I know, honey, you don't agree.
             (*Indicates painting*)
But this is our family tree.
Just wait till we're there, and you'll see —
Listen to me . . .
             (*Drifting off*)
Mama was smart . . .
Listen to Mama . . .
Children and art . . .
Children and art . . .
   (*She falls asleep and* ELAINE *crosses to her and wheels her*
   off. As they go:)
Goodbye, Mama.
             (GEORGE *looks at the painting for a moment*)

GEORGE: Connect, George. Connect . . .
             (GEORGE *exits; the painting flies out*)

   (*The island is once again revealed, though barely recog-*
   nizable as the trees have been replaced by high-rise build-
   ings. The only tree still visible is the one in front of which
   the OLD LADY *and* NURSE *sat.* DENNIS *kneels, studying his*
   blueprints. GEORGE *enters, camera in hand*)

GEORGE: Are you certain this is the best place for the
   Chromolume?

DENNIS: George, this is the largest clearing on La Grande
   Jatte.

GEORGE: Where's the still?

163

DENNIS: It has been built and should arrive tomorrow morning a few hours before the Chromolume. I wanted it here today, but they don't make deliveries on Sunday.

GEORGE: And fresh water for the cooling system?

DENNIS: We can draw it from the Seine. As for the electricity —

GEORGE: Did you see this tree?

DENNIS: No.

GEORGE: It could be the one in the painting.

DENNIS: Yes. It could.
    (GEORGE *hands* DENNIS *the camera and goes to the tree.* DENNIS *takes a picture of him in front of it*)

GEORGE: At least something is recognizable . . . Now, about the electricity?

DENNIS: The wind generator's over there.

GEORGE: You have been efficient as always.

DENNIS: Thank you.

GEORGE: I will miss working with you, Dennis.

DENNIS: Well, I can recommend some very capable people to help you with the Texas commission.

GEORGE: I turned it down.

DENNIS: What?

GEORGE: Dennis, why are you quitting?

DENNIS: I told you, I want —

GEORGE: I know what you told me! Why are you really leaving?

DENNIS: George. I love the Chromolumes. But I've helped you build the last five, and now I want to do something different.

164

GEORGE: I wish you had told me that in the first place.

DENNIS: I'm sorry.

GEORGE: Why do you think I turned down the commission? I don't want to do the same thing over and over again either.

DENNIS: There are other things you could do.

GEORGE: I know that. I just want to do something I care about.
(*Beat.* GEORGE *puts camera in pocket and pulls out* DOT*'s red book*)

DENNIS: I see you brought the red book.

GEORGE: Since Marie has died, I thought I would at least bring something of hers along.

DENNIS: Marie really wanted to make this trip.

GEORGE: I know.

DENNIS: I hope you don't mind, but I took a look at the book. It's very interesting.

GEORGE: It's just a grammar book, Dennis.

DENNIS (*Imploring*): Not that part. The notes in the back.
(GEORGE *leafs through it to the back*)
Well, we just have to wait for it to get dark. I'm not certain about the ambient light.

GEORGE: You go, Dennis. I'd like to be alone actually.

DENNIS: Are you sure?

GEORGE: Yeah. I'll see you back at the hotel.
(*He sits on the ground*)

DENNIS (*Begins to exit*): George. I look forward to seeing what you come up with next.

GEORGE (*Smiling*): You're not the only one, Dennis.

(DENNIS *exits. Music.* GEORGE *sings, leafing through the
book, reading*)
"Charles has a book . . ."
                    (*Turns a page*)
"Charles shows them his crayons . . ."
                    (*Turns back a few pages*)
"Marie has the ball of Charles . . ."
                (*Turns the book to read writing in the margin*)
"Good for Marie . . ."
           (*Smiles at the coincidence of the name, turns a page*)
"Charles misses his ball . . ."
                    (*Looks up*)
George misses Marie . . .
George misses a lot . . .
George is alone.

George looks around.
He sees the park.
It is depressing.
George looks ahead.
George sees the dark.
George is afraid.
Where are the people
Out strolling on Sunday?

George looks within:
George is adrift.
George goes by guessing.
George looks behind:
He had a gift.
When did it fade?
You wanted people out
Strolling on Sunday —
Sorry, Marie . . .
               (*Looks again at the name in the book*)
See George remember how George used to be,

166

Stretching his vision in every direction.
See George attempting to see a connection
When all he can see
Is maybe a tree —

(*Humorously*)

The family tree —
Sorry, Marie . . .

George is afraid.
George sees the park.
George sees it dying.
George too may fade,
Leaving no mark,
Just passing through.
Just like the people
Out strolling on Sunday . . .

George looks around.
George is alone.
No use denying
George is aground.
George has outgrown
What he can do.
George would have liked to see
People out strolling on Sunday . . .

(DOT *appears.* GEORGE *looks up and discovers her. He stands*)

DOT: I almost did not recognize you without your beard. You have my book.

GEORGE: Your book?

DOT: Yes.

GEORGE: It is a little difficult to understand.

DOT: Well, I was teaching myself. My writing got much better. I worked very hard. I made certain that Marie learned right away.

167

GEORGE (*Looks at the book*): Marie . . .

DOT: It is good to see you. Not that I ever forgot you, George. You gave me so much.

GEORGE: What did I give you?

DOT: Oh, many things. You taught me about concentration. At first I thought that meant just being still, but I was to understand it meant much more. You meant to tell me to be where I was — not some place in the past or future. I worried too much about tomorrow. I thought the world could be perfect. I was wrong.

GEORGE: What else?

DOT: Oh, enough about me. What about you? Are you working on something new?

GEORGE: No. I am not working on anything new.
(*Music begins*)

DOT: That is not like you, George.

GEORGE (*Sings*):
I've nothing to say.

DOT: You have many things . . .

GEORGE:
Well, nothing that's not been said.

DOT (*Sings*):
Said by you, though, George . . .

GEORGE:
I do not know where to go.

DOT:
And nor did I.

GEORGE:
I want to make things that count,

168

Things that will be new . . .

DOT (*Overlapping*):
    I did what I had to do:

GEORGE (*Overlapping*):
    What am I to do?

DOT:
    Move on.

    Stop worrying where you're going —
    Move on.
    If you can know where you're going,
    You've gone.
    Just keep moving on.

    I chose, and my world was shaken —
    So what?
    The choice may have been mistaken,
    The choosing was not.
    You have to move on.

    Look at what you want,
    Not at where you are,
    Not at what you'll be.
    Look at all the things you've done for me:
    Opened up my eyes,
    Taught me how to see,
    Notice every tree —

GEORGE:
    . . . Notice every tree . . .

DOT:
    Understand the light —

GEORGE:
    . . . Understand the light . . .

169

DOT:

Concentrate on now —

GEORGE:

I want to move on.
I want to explore the light.
I want to know how to get through,
Through to something new,
Something of my own —

GEORGE *and* DOT:

Move on.
Move on.

DOT:

Stop worrying if your vision
Is new.
Let others make that decision —
They usually do.
You keep moving on.

(*Simultaneously*)

DOT:	GEORGE
Look at what you've done,	(*Looking around*):
	. . . Something in the light,
Then at what you want,	Something in the sky,
Not at where you are,	In the grass,
What you'll be.	Up behind the trees . . .
Look at all the things	
You gave to me.	Things I hadn't looked at
Let me give to you	Till now:
Something in return.	Flower on your hat.
I would be so pleased . . .	And your smile.

GEORGE:

And the color of your hair.
And the way you catch the light . . .
And the care . . .

170

And the feeling . . .
And the life
Moving on . . .

DOT:
We've always belonged
Together!

GEORGE *and* DOT:
We will always belong
Together!

DOT:
Just keep moving on.

Anything you do,
Let it come from you.
Then it will be new.
Give us more to see . . .
> (*Speaks*)

You never cared what anyone thought. That upset me at the time because I wanted you to care what *I* thought.

GEORGE: I'm sure that I did.

DOT: I am sure that you did, too.

GEORGE: Dot.
> (*He takes the book to her*)

Why did you write these words?

DOT: They are your words, George. The ones you muttered so often when you worked.

GEORGE (*Reads slowly*):
"Order."
> (*Chord.* OLD LADY *enters*)

OLD LADY: George. Is that you?
> (GEORGE *turns to her. He looks back to* DOT, *who smiles, then back to the* OLD LADY)

171

GEORGE: Yes.

OLD LADY: Tell me! Is this place as you expected it?

GEORGE: What?

OLD LADY: The park, of course.

GEORGE: Somewhat.

OLD LADY: Go on.

GEORGE: Well, the greens are a little darker. The sky a little greyer. Mud tones in the water.

OLD LADY (*Disappointed*): Well, yes, I suppose —

GEORGE: But the air is rich and full of light.

OLD LADY: Good.
> (*Chord. As the* OLD LADY *leaves,* GEORGE *reads the next word:*)

GEORGE: "Design."
> (*Music begins: "Sunday." The downstage right building begins to rise. The* CELESTES *appear and begin to cross the stage*)

"Tension."
> (*Two buildings rise stage right and left. More characters from the painting appear and begin to promenade*)

"Composition."
> (*Building rises*)

"Balance."
> (*Buildings rise. The stage is filled by the characters from the painting*)

"Light."
> (*The large building in the back rises*)

Dot. I cannot read this word.

DOT: "Harmony."

ALL
(*Sing*):
Sunday,
By the blue
Purple yellow red water
On the green
Purple yellow red grass,
As we pass
Through arrangements of
  shadows
Towards the verticals of trees
Forever
  (*All bow to* GEORGE)
By the blue
Purple yellow red water
On the green
Orange violet mass
Of the grass . . .

GEORGE
(*Reading again, struggling
  with the words*):
"So much love in his words
. . . forever with his colors
. . . how George looks . . .
he can look forever . . . what
does he see? . . . his eyes so
dark and shiny. . . so careful
. . . so exact. . . ."
  (DOT *takes* GEORGE *by the arm
  and turns him to the group*)

DOT:
  In our perfect park . . .

GEORGE:
  Made of flecks of light
  And dark . . .

ALL (*Except* GEORGE *and* DOT):
  And parasols . . .
  People strolling through the trees
  Of a small suburban park
  On an island in the river
  On an ordinary Sunday . . .
    (*The* COMPANY *has settled generally in the areas that they
    occupy in the painting*)
  Sunday . . .

173

(All begin to leave very slowly, except DOT, *who remains downstage with* GEORGE)

Sunday . . .

*(*DOT *leaves* GEORGE, *crossing upstage into the park; she turns toward* GEORGE. *The white canvas drop descends)*

GEORGE *(Reading from the book)*: "White. A blank page or canvas. His favorite. So many possibilities . . . "

(He looks up and sees DOT *disappearing behind the white canvas. Lights fade to black)*

Set designs and sketches by Tony Straiges

Two models of the set

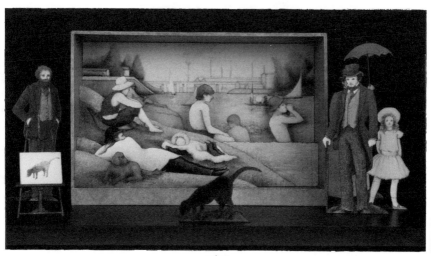

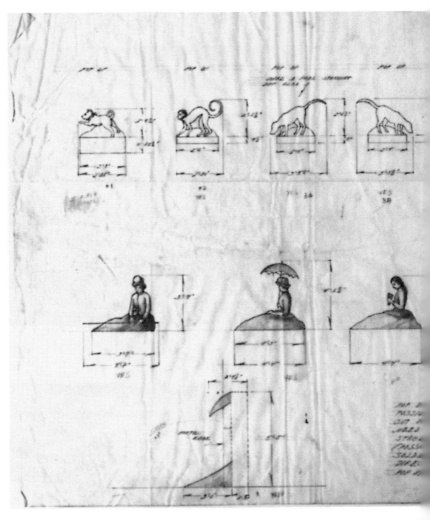

Blueprint for various of the onstage "pop-ups"
of characters and animals in the painting

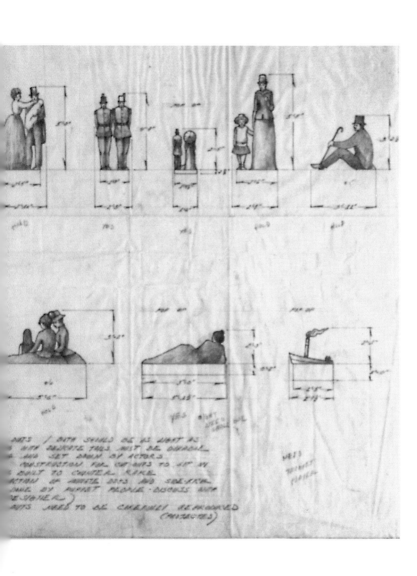

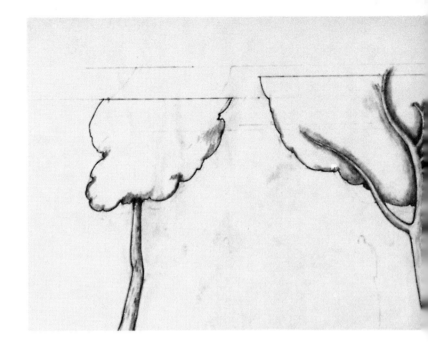

Sketches of scenic elements for Act I

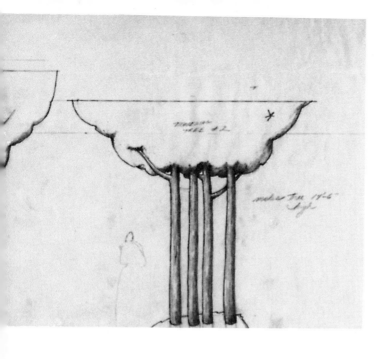

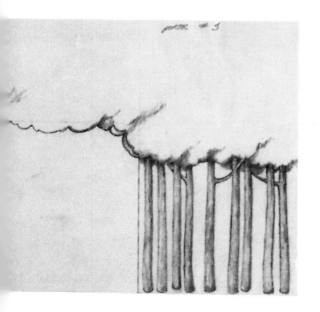

179

One of several working paintings (see pages 100-10)
showing the painting in progress

2

14' 8"

4"

Costume sketches by Patricia Zipprodt

Dot

182

Costume for Dot's dress
with bustle (*left*) and
(*below*) the same dress
with the bustle moved
to the front to create her
pregnant condition

183

Costume sketches by Ann Hould-Ward

Louis

Celeste #1

Companion and Soldier

ADDITIONAL LYRICS
with Commentary by Stephen Sondheim

"Yoo-Hoo!"

"Yoo-Hoo!" was sung in Scene I [at the place where the dialogue now starts on page 27].

(*Music. Laughter from stage right. A wagon tracks in. The sky backdrop lifts, revealing a large likeness of Seurat's "Une Baignade Asnières." The* BOY IN THE WATER *[foreground] and the* YOUNG MAN ON THE BANK *are real, as is the* PERVERT *[the man lying down]. The others are cut-outs in perspective. All direct a loud Bronx cheer at the island across the water. The* BOY *laughs, then turns to the others. He barks and yelps at the island, then laughs again. The* YOUNG MAN *echoes his laughter dull-wittedly*)

BOY (*Loudly, through cupped hands, sings*):
  Yoo-hoo! Big and fat!
  Who you think you're staring at?
            (*Stares exaggeratedly*)
  In about a minute flat
  We're all coming over to get you!
      (*He splashes water at the island. The* PERVERT *mutters something to the* BOY, *who nods delightedly and laughs*)
  Yoo-hoo! Kinky beard!
  Everybody knows you're weird!
            (YOUNG MAN *laughs while* PERVERT *mutters*)

PERVERT:
  How'd you like your picture smeared?

BOY:
  Yeah, how'd you like your picture smeared?

ALL:
  We're coming right over to get you!
      (BOY *makes menacing noises while the* YOUNG MAN *laughs*)

189

BOY (*turning to his audience*): Watch this.
                    (*Flails as if drowning*)

PERVERT *and* YOUNG MAN:
  Nursie! Nursie!
  Help, he's drowning!
                    (*Drowning sounds*)
  Mercy! Nursie!

BOY:
  I'm not clowning!
                    (NURSE *and* DOT *are alarmed*)

PERVERT *and* YOUNG MAN:
  Can't you see he's drowning?
      (BOY *makes horrifying drowning sounds and disappears*
      underwater, struggling; as the NURSE *and* GEORGE *move,*
      he suddenly pops up again)

BOY:
  Na-Na-Na-Ni-Na-Na!
      (*Belches gigantically;* PERVERT *mutters to him; speaks*)
  Huh?
      (*The* PERVERT *mutters more fully, explaining.* YOUNG MAN
      laughs first, then the BOY, *nodding. He whistles sexily,*
      sings)
  Yoo-hoo! Lady, dear!
  Who are you hiding in the rear?

PERVERT:
  Would you like a volunteer?

YOUNG MAN:
  Why don't you come over here?
                    (*The* PERVERT *mutters*)

BOY:
  Feeling weary, dear?

BOY *and* PERVERT:

Don't you worry, dearie,

ALL:

We're

Coming right over — !

(GEORGE *gestures; the* BOY, *the* YOUNG MAN *and the* PER-
VERT *freeze into the familiar tableau as a frame comes in
around them.* JULES *and* YVONNE *stroll on and examine
the picture, laughing*)

"Soldiers and Girls" and "The One on the Left"

*"Soldiers and Girls" was replaced by "The One on the Left,"
which in turn was cut down to the fragment that now remains on
pages 63-65.*

"Soldiers and Girls"

SOLDIER (*Sudden and loud*):
> Mademoiselles,
> I and my friend
> We are but soldiers —
>> (*Listens to sidekick*)
> Passing the time
> In between wars,
> However we may.

CELESTE #2:
> Careful, he's peculiar.

CELESTE #1:
> How is he peculiar?

CELESTE #2:
> Soldiers are peculiar.

SOLDIER:
> And after a week spent
> Mostly indoors
> With nothing but soldiers,
> May we venture to say:
>> (*Softening his ardor at a nudge from the other soldier*)
> It's a glorious day.

CELESTE #2:
> Wasn't that peculiar?

CELESTE #1:

No, it's not peculiar.

CELESTE #2:

Something is peculiar.
Shouldn't we be going?

CELESTE #1:

No, will you be quiet?

SOLDIER:

Sundays were made for soldiers and girls,
Don't you agree?
Sundays were made for medals
And ribbons arrayed with red sashes,
Buckles and braid,
And sabres —
And girls.

Sundays were meant for helmets and plumes,
Mademoiselles,
Meant for salutes
And epaulettes,
Glistening boots,
The heady perfumes
Of horses and grooms —
And beautiful girls!

(*Very loud*)

Mademoiselles!
I and my friend
Have a suggestion!

CELESTE #2:

Anyone can see that
That man is peculiar.

SOLDIER:

I and my friend

193

Wish to be friends
With you and your friend.

CELESTE #1:
See, he's very friendly.

CELESTE #2:
Yes, he's very friendly.
That's what is peculiar.

SOLDIER:
Only just now
I said to my friend
Of you and your friend,
"I suspect they are friends."

CELESTE #1:
Both of them are perfect.

CELESTE #2:
You can have the other.

CELESTE #1:
I don't want the other.

CELESTE #2:
I don't want the other either.

SOLDIER:
And, see, you are friends!

CELESTE #1 *and* #2:
What can be the harm in
Strolling in the park with
Soldiers even if they *are* peculiar?

SOLDIER:
And we shall be friends.

SOLDIER, CELESTE #1 *and* #2:
Sundays were made for soldiers and girls.

194

SOLDIER:

Mademoiselles,
Sundays were made for medals —
   (*Looks expectantly at* CELESTE #1, *who picks up her cue*)

CELESTE #1:

And ribbons arrayed with red sashes —
                    (*Nudges* CELESTE #2)

CELESTE #2:

Buckets and braid —

CELESTE #1 (*Whispers*): Buckles!

SOLDIER:

And sabres —
   (*Looks at sidekick, who apparently conveys something; speaks*)
Right!
                         (*Sings*)
Sundays were made for banners and bells,
Don't you agree?
Made for whatever sparkles,
                    (*With meaning*)
Whatever is fresh and sweet,
                    (CELESTES *giggle*)
Everything casting colorful spells:
For beaches and shells
                    (CELESTES *hum*)
And scarlet lapels
                    (*Inhales*)
And vigorous smells —
And soldiers!
              (*At a nudge from the sidekick*)
And mademoiselles!

CELESTE #1 (*Aside*):
  Both of them are perfect.

CELESTE #2:
  You can have the other.

CELESTE #1:
  I don't want the other.

CELESTE #2:
  I don't want the other either.

SOLDIER:
  Mademoiselles,
  I and my friend,
  We are but soldiers —
    (*Rumble from his* COMPANION*;* SOLDIER *raises hand to
    quiet him*)
  Passing the time
  In between wars
  For weeks at an end.

CELESTE #2 (*Aside*):
  Shouldn't we be going?

CELESTE #1:
  No, will you be quiet?

CELESTE #2:
  Something is peculiar —

SOLDIER:
  And after a week
  Spent mostly indoors
  With nothing but soldiers,
  Ladies, I and my friend
  Trust we will not offend,
  Which we'd never intend,

196

By suggesting we spend —

BOTH CELESTES (*Excited*):
Oh, spend —

SOLDIER:
— This magnificent Sunday —

BOTH CELESTES (*A bit defeated*):
Oh, Sunday —

SOLDIER:
— With you and your friend.

CELESTE #2 (*Aside, to* CELESTE #1):
The one on the right seems quite attached.

CELESTE #1 (*Looking over, then back*):
As well as scratched.

SOLDIER (*Aside, to* COMPANION):
Admit it, old man, we're not badly matched.

ALL (*To themselves, shrugging*):
It's certainly fine for Sunday.

SOLDIER (*To* COMPANION):
The one on the left seems quite subdued.

CELESTE #2 (*As* CELESTE #1 *tries to elbow her over to the other side*):
I'm not in the mood.

CELESTE #1 (*To* CELESTE #2):
You're ruining things and we're being rude —

ALL (*Enthusiastically, to each other*):
It's certainly fine for Sunday!
(*During the next section, as they all march around, both* CELESTES *fight for position*)

SOLDIER *and* CELESTE #1 (*Aside, to their partners*):
My only advice
Is don't think twice.

SOLDIER (*To* CELESTE #1):
  Would you care for an ice?

BOTH CELESTES:
  Oh, an ice would be nice!

CELESTE #2 (*To* CELESTE #1):
  Will they buy us a drink?

SOLDIER (*To* COMPANION):
  Are they virgins, you think?

ALL (*To each other*):
  It's certainly fine for Sunday!

CELESTE #2 (*To* CELESTE #1, *referring to* COMPANION):
  Is that a mustache
  Or just a gash?

CELESTE #1 (*To* SOLDIER):
  What a beautiful sash!

SOLDIER (*To* COMPANION):
  Did you bring any cash?

CELESTE #1 (*To* CELESTE #2):
  The buckles and braid —

CELESTE #2:
  The gold brocade —

CELESTE #1:
  The boots —

CELESTE #2:
  The blade — !

SOLDIER:
  Shall we head for the glade?

CELESTE #1 (*Excited, aside*):
  Heading for the shadows — !

198

CELESTE #2 (*Also excited, but wary*):
Anything can happen —

CELESTE #1:
Wonder what they're planning.

CELESTE #2 (*Alarmed*):
What they're planning?

CELESTE #1:
What they're planning later on!

SOLDIER (*To* COMPANION):
The one on the right gave you a look —
Let's hope she can cook.

BOTH CELESTES (*Aside*):
Taking us to dinner —
Maybe to the Follies — !
Anyhow, it's certainly fine for Sunday!

CELESTE #1:
The one on the right is odd, it's true,
But what can we do?

SOLDIER (*To* COMPANION):
The one on the left —

CELESTE #1:
You're as odd as he —

SOLDIER:
— Has great esprit —

CELESTE #2:
I don't agree —

SOLDIER *and* CELESTE #1:
The one on the left is right for me —
        (*They switch positions so that* CELESTE #2 *has the* COMPANION)
So the one on the right is left for you.

MAJOR PRODUCTIONS

Sunday in the Park with George was first presented in a workshop production for 25 performances by Playwrights Horizons (André Bishop, Artistic Director; Paul Daniels, Managing Director; Ira Weitzman, Musical Theater Program Director), in association with the Herrick Theater Foundation, at Playwrights Horizons, New York City, July 6–July 31, 1983, with the following cast:

(*In order of appearance*)

ACT I

GEORGE, *an artist*	Mandy Patinkin
DOT, *his mistress*	Bernadette Peters
OLD LADY	Carmen Mathews
HER NURSE	Judith Moore
FRANZ, *a coachman*	Brent Spiner
BOY IN THE WATER	Bradley Kane
YOUNG MAN ON THE BANK	Kelsey Grammer
PERVERT	William Parry
LOUISE, *a little girl*	Danielle Ferland
JULES, *another artist*	Ralph Byers
CLARISSE, *his wife*	Christine Baranski
BOATMAN	William Parry
LOUIS, *a baker*	Kevin Marcum
CELESTE #1, *a shopgirl*	Melanie Vaughan
CELESTE #2, *another shopgirl*	Mary Elizabeth Mastrantonio
BETTE, *a cook*	Nancy Opel
SOLDIER	Kelsey Grammer
MR.	Kurt Knudson
MRS.	Judith Moore

ACT II

GEORGE, *a performance artist*	Mandy Patinkin
JED	Brent Spiner
DEE, *George's girlfriend*	Nancy Opel
ALEX	Kelsey Grammer
ANNETTE, *George's grandmother*	Bernadette Peters
NAOMI	Melanie Vaughan
ROBERT BLACKMUN, *the museum director*	Kurt Knudson
BILLIE GHERKIN, *a patroness of the arts*	Carmen Mathews
HARRIET PAWLING, *a patroness of the arts*	Judith Moore
WAITER	Ross Wassermann
CHARLES GREEN, *a museum curator*	William Parry
ALAN CASH, *museum benefactor*	Kevin Marcum
LINDA CASH, *his wife*	Mary Elizabeth Mastrantonio
BLAIR DANIELS, *an art critic*	Christine Baranski
WAITRESS	Johnna Murray

Directed by James Lapine
Set Design by Tony Straiges
Costume Design by Patricia Zipprodt *and* Ann Hould-Ward
Lighting Design by Richard Nelson
Sound Design by Scott Lehrer
Musical Director, Paul Gemignani

NOTE: It was only for the last three performances of the workshop production that the second act was presented.

MUSICAL NUMBERS

ACT I

"Sunday in the Park with George"	DOT
"Yoo-Hoo!"	BOY, YOUNG MAN, PERVERT
"No Life"	JULES, CLARISSE
"Color and Light"	DOT, GEORGE
"Gossip"	CELESTE #1, CELESTE #2, BOATMAN NURSE, OLD LADY, JULES, CLARISSE
"The Day Off"	GEORGE, SPOT, FIFI, NURSE, FRANZ, BETTE, BOATMAN, SOLDIER, CLARISSE, LOUISE, CELESTE #1, CELESTE #2
"Everybody Loves Louis"	DOT
"Soldiers and Girls"	SOLDIER, CELESTE #1, CELESTE #2
"Finishing the Hat"	GEORGE
"Beautiful"	OLD LADY, GEORGE
"Sunday"	COMPANY

ACT II

"It's Hot Up Here"	DOT, CLARISSE, LOUISE, FRANZ, NURSE, CELESTE #1, CELESTE #2, BETTE, JULES, SOLDIER, OLD LADY, BOATMAN
Performance Art Piece	GEORGE, JED, DEE, ALEX, ANNETTE, NAOMI
"Have to Keep Them Humming"	HARRIET, BILLIE, BLACKMUN, GREEN, NAOMI, ALEX, JED, LINDA, ALAN, GEORGE
"Sunday" (reprise)	COMPANY

205

Sunday in the Park with George was presented by The Shubert Organization and Emanuel Azenberg, by arrangement with Playwrights Horizons, at the Booth Theatre, New York City, on May 2, 1984, with the following cast:

(In order of appearance)

ACT I

GEORGE, *an artist*	Mandy Patinkin
DOT, *his mistress*	Bernadette Peters
AN OLD LADY	Barbara Bryne
HER NURSE	Judith Moore
FRANZ, *a servant*	Brent Spiner
A BOY *bathing in the river*	Danielle Ferland
A YOUNG MAN *sitting on the bank*	Nancy Opel
A MAN *lying on the bank*	Cris Groenendaal
JULES, *another artist*	Charles Kimbrough
YVONNE, *his wife*	Dana Ivey
A BOATMAN	William Parry
CELESTE #1	Melanie Vaughan
CELESTE #2	Mary D'Arcy
LOUISE, *the daughter of Jules and Yvonne*	Danielle Ferland
FRIEDA, *a cook*	Nancy Opel
LOUIS, *a baker*	Cris Groenendaal
A SOLDIER	Robert Westenberg
A MAN *with bicycle*	John Jellison
A LITTLE GIRL	Michele Rigan
A WOMAN *with baby carriage*	Sue Anne Gershenson
MR.	Kurt Knudson
MRS.	Judith Moore

ACT II

GEORGE, *an artist*	Mandy Patinkin
MARIE, *his grandmother*	Bernadette Peters
DENNIS, *a technician*	Brent Spiner
BOB GREENBERG, *the museum director*	Charles Kimbrough
NAOMI EISEN, *a composer*	Dana Ivey
HARRIET PAWLING, *a patron of the arts*	Judith Moore
BILLY WEBSTER, *her friend*	Cris Groenendaal
A PHOTOGRAPHER	Sue Anne Gershenson
A MUSEUM ASSISTANT	John Jellison
CHARLES REDMOND, *a visiting curator*	William Parry
ALEX, *an artist*	Robert Westenberg
BETTY, *an artist*	Nancy Opel
LEE RANDOLPH, *the museum's publicist*	Kurt Knudson
BLAIR DANIELS, *an art critic*	Barbara Bryne
A WAITRESS	Melanie Vaughan
ELAINE	Mary D'Arcy

Directed by James Lapine
Scenery by Tony Straiges
Costumes by Patricia Zipprodt *and* Ann Hould-Ward
Lighting Design by Richard Nelson
Special Effects by Bran Ferren
Movement by Randolyn Zinn
Sound by Tom Morse
Hair and Makeup by Lo Presto/Allen
Musical Direction by Paul Gemignani
Orchestrations by Michael Starobin

207

The following musical numbers were deleted prior to the May 2, 1984 opening: "*Yoo-Hoo!*" "*Soldiers and Girls,*" "*Have to Keep Them Humming*"

Sunday in the Park with George gave its first performance in New York City at the Booth Theatre, where it began previews on April 2, 1984, opened on May 2nd and closed on October 12, 1985 after 604 performances and 35 previews.

AWARDS

Pulitzer Prize — Drama (1985)

New York Drama Critics Circle Award — Best Musical

Tony Awards: Best Scenic Design (Tony Straiges) and Best Lighting (Richard Nelson). Also received Tony nominations for Best Musical, Best Book of a Musical (James Lapine), Best Music and Lyrics (Stephen Sondheim), Best Direction of a Musical (James Lapine), Best Actor in a Musical (Mandy Patinkin), Best Actress in a Musical (Bernadette Peters), Best Featured Actress in a Musical (Dana Ivey), Best Costume Design (Patricia Zipprodt and Ann Hould-Ward).

Sunday in the Park with George was first presented in London by the Royal National Theatre in repertory at the Lyttelton Theatre on March 15, 1990 for a limited engagement of 117 performances, with the following cast:

(*In order of appearance*)

ACT I

GEORGE, *an artist*	Philip Quast
DOT, *his mistress*	Maria Friedman
AN OLD LADY	Sheila Ballantine
HER NURSE	Nuala Willis
FRANZ, *servant to Jules and Yvonne*	Michael O'Connor
BOY BATHER	Keir Charles or Samuel Woodward
SMALL BOY BATHERS	Christopher Line, Marc Bellamy or Marco Williamson, James Nyman
JULES, *another artist*	Gary Raymond
YVONNE, *his wife*	Nyree Dawn Porter
A BOATMAN	Michael Attwell
CELESTE #1	Megan Kelly
CELESTE #2	Clare Burt
LOUIS, *a baker*	Aneirin Huws
A SOLDIER	Nicolas Colicos
LOUISE, *daughter to Jules and Yvonne*	Naomi Kerbel or Ann Gosling
FRIEDA, *Jules and Yvonne's cook, wife to Franz*	Di Botcher
MAN PLAYING THE HORN	Barry Atkinson
DANCING GIRL	Antonio Boyd or Emily Sault
WOMAN LOOKING FOR A GLOVE	Ellen van Schuylenburch
MR. & MRS., *an American couple*	Matt Zimmerman and Vivienne Martin

ACT II

GEORGE, *an artist*	Philip Quast
MARIE, *his grandmother*	Maria Friedman
DENNIS, *a technician*	Michael O'Connor
BOB GREENBERG, *the museum director*	Gary Raymond
NAOMI EISEN, *a composer*	Nyree Dawn Porter
HARRIET PAWLING, *a patron of the arts*	Nuala Willis
BILLIE WEBSTER, *her friend*	Vivienne Martin
CHARLES REDMOND, *a visiting curator*	Matt Zimmerman
ALEX, *an artist*	Nicolas Colicos
BETTY, *an artist*	Clare Burt
LEE RANDOLPH, *the museum's publicist*	Michael Attwell
BLAIR DANIELS, *an art critic*	Sheila Ballantine
ELAINE, *George's former wife*	Di Botcher
CHROMOLUME PERFORMERS	Barry Atkinson, Aneirin Huws, Megan Kelly, Ellen van Schuylenburch
A WAITRESS	Buffy Davis
A PHOTOGRAPHER	Simon Fielder
GUESTS	Stephen Hanley, Erika Vincent

Directed by Steven Pimlott
Designed by Tom Cairns
Lighting by Wolfgang Gobbel
Orchestrations by Michael Starobin
Musical Direction by Jeremy Sams
Choreographer, Aletta Collins
Chromolume #7, Martin Duncan
Sound, Mike Clayton, Paul Groothius
Conductor, John Jansson

Sunday in the Park with George was presented by Michael Brandman and Emanuel Azenberg, in association with The Shubert Organization and American Playhouse, on cable television's "Broadway on Showtime" series on February 18, 1986, and subsequently on "American Playhouse" (PBS) on June 16, 1986, with the following cast:

GEORGE, *an artist*	Mandy Patinkin
DOT/MARIE	Bernadette Peters
JULES/BOB GREENBERG	Charles Kimbrough
OLD LADY/BLAIR DANIELS	Barbara Bryne
YVONNE/NAOMI EISEN	Dana Ivey
CELESTE #2/ELAINE	Mary D'Arcy
WOMAN/PHOTOGRAPHER	Sue Anne Gershenson
LOUIS/BILLY WEBSTER	Cris Groenendaal
MAN/PARTY GUEST	John Jellison
MR./PUBLICIST	Frank Kopyc
NURSE/MRS./HARRIET PAWLING	Judith Moore
FRIEDA/BETTY	Nancy Opel
BOATMAN/CHARLES REDMOND	William Parry
LOUISE	Natalie Polizzie
GIRL	Michele Rigan
FRANZ/DENNIS	Brent Spiner
CELESTE #1/WAITRESS	Melanie Vaughan
SOLDIER/ALEX	Robert Westenberg

Produced by Iris Merlis
Executive in Charge of Production, Greg Sills
Directed for Television by Terry Hughes
Directed for the Stage by James Lapine
Musical Director and Conductor, Paul Gemignani
Orchestrations by Michael Starobin

211

Scenery by Tony Straiges
Costumes by Patricia Zipprodt *and* An Hould-Ward
Lighting Design by Richard Nelson
Lighting Consultant, Bill Klages
Special Effects by Bran Ferren
Movement by Randolyn Zinn
Sound by Tom Morse

The television production was taped October 21-25, 1985 at the Booth Theatre shortly after the close of the Broadway production and with all but two members (Kurt Knudson and Danielle Ferland) of the original Broadway cast. This production is available on video cassette: Lorimar Home Video 370/Image Entertainment DG(S) ID5151.

SELECTED DISCOGRAPHY

* Original Broadway Cast Recording (1984)
    RCA Records
        LP HBC1-5042 (S)
        Cassette HBE1-5042
        CD   RCD1-5042

A Collector's Sondheim (1985)
    RCA Records
        LP CRL4-5359 (S); 4 record set
        Cassette   CRK4-5359; 4 tape set
        CD RCD3-5480; 3 disc set
    Includes: *"Children and Art"*—Bernadette Peters, Mandy Patinkin;
        "Move On"—Bernadette Peters, Mandy Patinkin (both
        tracks from original Broadway cast recording)

Sondheim (1985)
    Book-of-the-Month Records
        LP 81-7515 (S); 3 record set
        Cassette   91-7516; 2 tape set
        CD 11-7517; 2 disc set
    Includes: *"Finishing the Hat"*—Cris Groenendaal

The Broadway Album/Barbra Streisand (1985)
    Columbia Records
        LP OC 40092
        Cassette OCT 40092
        CD CK 40092
    Includes: *"Putting It Together"* (with Sondheim's slightly revised
        lyric)

Symphonic Sondheim/Don Sebesky Conducts The London
Symphony Orchestra (1990)
    WEA Records (London)
        LP 9031–72 119–1
        Cassette 9031–72 119–4
        CD 9031–72 119–2
    Includes: *"Finishing the Hat"*

* Winner of the Grammy Award for Best Original Cast Show Album

Stephen Sondheim wrote the music and lyrics for *A Funny Thing Happened on the Way to the Forum* (1962), *Anyone Can Whistle* (1964), *Company* (1970), *Follies* (1971), *A Little Night Music* (1973), *The Frogs* (1974), *Pacific Overtures* (1976), *Sweeney Todd, the Demon Barber of Fleet Street* (1979), *Merrily We Roll Along* (1981), *Sunday in the Park with George* (1984), *Into the Woods* (1986) and *Assassins* (1990), the lyrics for *West Side Story* (1957, music by Leonard Bernstein), *Gypsy* (1959, music by Jule Styne) and *Do I Hear a Waltz?* (1965, music by Richard Rodgers), and additional lyrics for a new production of *Candide* (1973, music by Leonard Bernstein). He provided incidental music for the plays *The Girls of Summer* (1956), *Invitation to a March* (1961), *Twigs* (1971) and *The Enclave* (1973). He wrote the music and lyrics for the television production *Evening Primrose* (1966), composed the film scores for *Stavisky* (1974) and *Reds* (1981), wrote songs for the motion pictures *The Seven Percent Solution* (1976) and *Dick Tracy* (1990) and co-authored the film *The Last of Sheila* (1973). He won Tony Awards for his scores for *Company, Follies, A Little Night Music, Sweeney Todd* and *Into the Woods*, and all of these musicals won the New York Drama Critics Circle Award for Best Musical, as did *Pacific Overtures* and *Sunday in the Park with George*, the latter also receiving the Pulitzer Prize in 1985. Mr. Sondheim is on the Council of the Dramatists Guild, having served as its president from 1973 to 1981, was elected to the American Academy and Institute of Arts and Letters in 1983, received the London Evening Standard Award in 1989 for his contribution to the musical theater, and in 1989 was named the first Visiting Professor of Contemporary Theatre at Oxford University.

James Lapine is a playwright and director who first became involved with the theater in the mid-seventies while working as a graphic designer at the Yale School of Drama, where he staged his interpretation of Gertrude Stein's *Photograph*. His plays include *Table Settings* and *Twelve Dreams*, and he wrote the books for the musicals *Sunday in the Park with George* and *Into the Woods*, all four of which he also directed. He was the director of William Finn's musical *March of the Falsettos* and co-author with Mr. Finn and director of its sequel, *Falsettoland* (both at Playwrights

Horizons), *A Midsummer Night's Dream* and *The Winter's Tale* (both for the New York Shakespeare Festival), and a new production of the Stephen Sondheim/George Furth musical *Merrily We Roll Along* (at the La Jolla Playhouse). He has recently directed his first feature film, *Impromptu.*

André Bishop is the Artistic Director of Playwrights Horizons in New York City, a theater company devoted to the support and development of American playwrights, composers, and lyricists and to the production of their work. Notable plays first produced there by Mr. Bishop include *Sister Mary Ignatius Explains It All For You* by Christopher Durang, *The Dining Room* by A. R. Gurney, *March of the Falsettos* by William Finn, among many others, and three Pulitzer Prize Winners—*Driving Miss Daisy* by Alfred Uhry, *The Heidi Chronicles* by Wendy Wasserstein, and, of course, *Sunday in the Park with George.*